SARAKHSĪ – HUGO GROTIUS

OF

THE MUSLIMS

THE DOCTRINE OF JURISTIC PREFERENCE

AND

THE

CONCEPTS OF TREATIES AND MUTUAL RELATIONS

by

HUSAIN KASSIM

SARAKHSĪ – HUGO GROTIUS

OF

THE MUSLIMS

THE DOCTRINE OF JURISTIC PREFERENCE

AND

THE

CONCEPTS OF TREATIES AND MUTUAL RELATIONS

by

HUSAIN KASSIM

AUSTIN & WINFIELD, PUBLISHERS
SAN FRANCISCO-LONDON

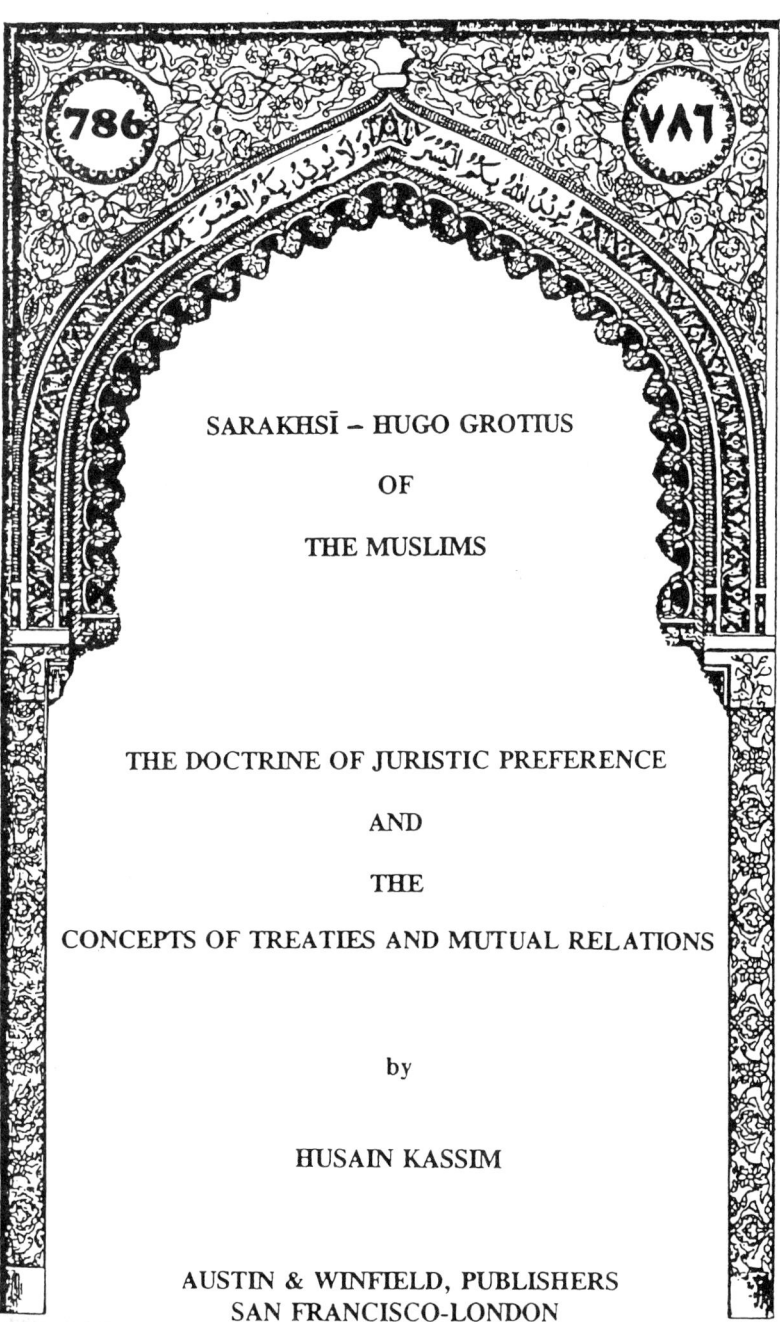

Library of Congress Cataloging-in-Publication Data

Kassim, Husain ,1939-

Sarakhsi : concept of treaties and the doctrine of juristic preference in Islamic jurisprudence / Husain Kassim

p. cm.

Includes bibliographical references and index.

ISBN 1-880921-90-1(cloth) : $74.95 - ISBN 1-880921-89-8 (pbk.): $54.95

1. Sarakhsi, Muhammad ibn Ahmad, 11th cent. 2. Islamic law--Interpretation and construction. 3. International law (Islamic law) 4. Religious minorities--Legal status, laws, etc.--Islamic countries. I. Title.

LAW <ISLAM 7 Kass 1994>
340.5'9--dc20 94-12579
CIP

Editorial Inquiries:
Austin & Winfield, Publishers
7831 Woodmont Avenue #345
Bethesda,MD. 20814
(301) 654-7335

To Order: (800) 99-AUSTIN

TABLE OF CONTENTS

PREFACE

The author's long-awaited research work now presented as **Sarakhsī--Hugo Grotius** of the Muslims on the doctrine of juristic preference (istiḥsān) is a welcome and much needed contribution toward the revival of the methodology in the Islamic social sciences and particularly in the Islamic system of law.

Dr. Kassim had already contributed an article on Sarakhsī 's methodological approach concerning the subject matter of treaties (muwāda'a) and mutual relations (mu'āmlāt) of Muslims with other nations in **The American Journal of Islamic Social Sciences** (Vol. 5, No. 2, 1988). At that time as an editor of the **Journal**, I was pleased to see Dr. Kassim devoting his research project to the Ḥanafī jurist Sarakhsī whose contributions regarding the doctrine of juristic preference and its application on the treaties and mutual relations of Muslims with other nations have been overlooked in the history of Islamic jurisprudence, especially as a methodological approach and its possible relevance to the modern day world of Islam.

It needs to be noticed that at present considerable attention is being paid in academic world to the various aspects of Islamic jurisprudence and especially to the Mālikī school of thought, but somehow there is a dearth of research work on the Ḥanafī school of thought, especially on the doctrine of juristic preference. This book meets this short coming.

In addition to that, the author has expounded extensively, particularly in Chapter Six of his book, on the historical development of the juristic method of reasoning (ra'y) in Islamic jurisprudence and placed properly the vital role of the Ḥanafī doctrine of istiḥsān (juristic preference) and the Mālikī doctrine of istiṣlāḥ (consideration of what is beneficial or expedient) and brought out the relevance of Sarakhsī's doctrine of istiḥsān (juristic preference) in relation to the worldly affairs of Muslims with other nations. This contribution of Sarakhsī as interpreted and developed by the author may become a guide toward proper advancement of the Islamic system of law, not only in theory, but also in practice.

I wish, Sarakhsī, Hugo Grotius of the Muslims, as Dr. Kassim names him comes to visibility as a treasure of the Muslim legacy in Islamic jurisprudence.

Sayyid M. Sayeed, Editor-in-Chief
The American Journal of
Islamic Social Sciences

GENERAL NOTE

Throughout the entire book, the Muslim calendar year of Hijra (A.H.) is given first and the Gregorian calendar year (A.D.) follows with an oblique stroke. Occassionally, a Muslim calendar year will fall within one Christian solar year, but usually there will be some overlapping between them.

In rendering the Qur'ānic verses into English, we have followed Yusuf Ali's translation, except when necessary minor changes have been made.

When any Arabic term is used for the first time in this work, its equivalent in English is provided in parentheses. If the term is used quite frequently, then afterwards either only the Arabic term is used, or only its equivalent in English. For example, with the terms qiyās (systematic reasoning) and istiḥsān (juristic preference); sometimes only the Arabic terms qiyās and istiḥsān are used, while at other times, only their English equivalents.

ACKNOWLEDGMENTS

My thanks are due to many teachers, friends and students, but special thanks are due to Professor Babar Johansen of Free University of Berlin for the valuable suggestions and criticisms. I am particularly thankful to Dr. Ida Cook for reading the first draft of the manuscript and Silvia without whose help this camera ready copy of the Text would have not been possible; and, finally, my wife, Kulsoom who was patient enough to go through the whole process. Besides, my greatest gratitude is to the driving force behind this investigation:

"My life (nafs) is in this world (dunyā) and finding its
inward meaning (ma'ānī) is my goal".

INTRODUCTION

The focus of our present investigation is Sarakhsī's doctrine of juristic preference (istiḥsān) based on his **Uṣūl al-Fiqh, Mabsūṭ** and **Kitāb al-Muwāda'a** from his **Sharḥ al-Sayir al-Kabīr**. The main contentions which emerge as a result of the examination of Sarakhsī's works are as follows:

(i) Sarakhsī employs ra'y (juristic reasoning) in the form of istiḥsān as a valid and justifiable methodological approach to broaden the scope of Islamic jurisprudence.
(ii) Sarakhsī systematizes and analyzes the 'illa (effective reasoning) of the doctrine of istiḥsān (juristic preference) and develops it to its fullest taking into account the criticisms and objections raised against the validity of the doctrine of istiḥsān (juristic preference) in the historical development of Islamic jurisprudence. Before Sarakhsī, this task had not been accomplished quite completely by the Ḥanafī jurists of the past as it will become clear in the course of the present investigation.
(iii) Finally, Sarakhsī subjects the contents of muwāda'a (treaties), mu'āmalāt (mutual relations) of Muslims with other nations concerning the aḥkām al-dunyā (worldy affairs) in conjunction and juxtaposition with the doctrine of istiḥsān (juristic preference) and analyzes them vigorously from that standpoint, incorporating them within the proper focus and framework of sharī'a law in Islamic jurisprudence. These aspects of Sarakhsī's works and thoughts are discussed here briefly in the background of the controversy regarding the use of ra'y (juristic reasoning) in the form of the doctrine of istiḥsān (juristic preference) so that the reader may easily grasp what follows subsequently in the course of our investigation.

From the early stages of the development of Islamic jurisprudence, the prerogative status of the Qur'ān and Sunna as the sources of law was recognized and formed the basis of Islamic jurisprudence in all its aspects. In the beginning, the Muslim community was regulated in its affairs by the rules and regulations provided by these sources which became the guides of the Muslim community. With the expansion of Islam under the first Caliphs, the authorities entrusted with the administration of justice and control of religious affairs had in most cases to fall back on the exercise of ra'y (personal opinion). The recognition of ra'y as an approved source of law found expression in the instructions attributed to the Prophet and the early Caliphs which they gave to the officials who were sent to administer justice in the conquered provinces[1] and with this, the ra'y as a principle was given a systematic validity and the qiyās (what is here translated as the doctrine of systematic reasoning after Schacht[2] rather than what is usually translated as the analogy) became a methodological regulation. The doctrine of systematic reasoning (qiyās) as a principle of deduction based on reasoning (ra'y) became a popular element adopted as one of the constitutive sources for the deduction of laws.[3]

In the second half of the first century Hijra/early eighth century A.D., Islamic jurisprudence (fiqh) began to develop at the same time as the science of tradition ('ilm al-ḥadīth). This gave rise to rivalry between the traditionalists (ahl al-ḥadīth) and the rationalists (ahl al-ra'y).[4] In spite of this opposition, the ra'y employed in the form of qiyās found its place among the constitutive sources of Islamic jurisprudence by the ijmā' (general consensus) which is the third source of Islamic jurisprudence. The earliest founders of madhāhibs (schools of thought) compiled their manuals of law, either by oral communication like Abū Ḥanīfa (150 A.H./767 A.D.) or in writing, like Mālik bin Anas (179 A.H./795 A.D.), the founder of the Ḥijāzī school of thought who wrote corpus jurist **Muwaṭṭa'** which is the synthesis of the four roots (namely, the Qur'ān, Sunna, ijmā' and qiyās) of Islamic jurisprudence. Muḥammad bin Idrīs al-Shāfi'ī (204 A.H./767 A.D.) is probably the first to synthesize the method of reasoning and make use of it without undisputed prerogatives of the Scripture and traditions (aḥādīth). Aḥmad bin Ḥambal (241 A.H./855A.D.) makes concessions only under absolute necessity and tries to derive the laws from the traditions (aḥādīth).[5]

However, as shown by recent historical research, Islamic jurisprudence as a discipline in the technical sense came into prominence at the end of the first century Hijra/early eighth century A.D., as we find with the foundation of the four Islamic schools of thought; of those, Kūfa, Medina and Syria are known to us in detail. The differences among them were caused in the first place by geographical factors such as local variations in social conditions, customary law and practice, but they were not based on any noticeable disagreement on principles or methods.[6] Nonetheless, when it came to the use of raʾy as a methodology of reasoning for the derivation of the laws, they all used it in different forms and not to the same extent. Mālik, in his jurisprudence, gives preference to the ʿamal or Sunna (the actual practice in Medina) and to the traditions (aḥādīth). When these practices or traditions were not found to exist, he laid down the law independently and recognized the use of raʾy (reasoning) and it is considered as the istiṣlāḥ (consideration of what is beneficial or expedient maṣlaḥa or murāʿāt al-aṣlaḥ).[7] In the Ḥanafī school of thought, it was put on a firmer footing by Abū Yūsuf (182 A.H./798 A.D.) and Shaybānī (189 A.H./804 A.D.) by whom it was given a free reign and was used by him extensively. A certain amount of freedom was given for deviation from the usual methodology of qiyās by allowing practical considerations and it was called the istiḥsān (juristic preference).[8] By the same token, in the Shāfiʿī school of thought, the raʾy as the methodology of reasoning is used in the form of istiṣḥāb (the presumption of continuity of judicial or legal situation as it had existed previously, so long as there does not exist any evidence for its discontinuity).[9] Since the principle of istiṣḥāb as a method of reasoning is not a source for the derivation of new laws, it does not become disputable in the history of Islamic jurisprudence.

Thus, reduced to its naked form, the nub of the matter is the use of raʾy in the form of the doctrine of istiḥsān and the doctrine of istiṣlāḥ as the valid sources of law in Islamic jurisprudence. The jurists from the Ḥanafī school of thought defend the doctrine of istiḥsān by showing that the ʿilla (effective reasoning) employed in the doctrine is based on and connected with the aṣl (Origin); namely, the Qurʾān, Ḥadīth and ijmāʿ and the jurists from the Mālikī school of thought criticize it by pointing out that such is not the case. Hence, we have investigated Sarakhsī's doctrine of juristic preference solely from the aspect of ʿilla which is employed in the doctrine without dwelling extensively on the details on which these two doctrines differ from each other, since the issue centers around whether the ʿilla used in the doctrine of istiḥsān as a methodological reasoning (raʾy) is based on and connected with the aṣl (Origin).

Essentially, the framework of Sarakhsī's works is from the perspective of methodological reasoning (raʾy) in the form of the doctrine of qiyās and the doctrine of istiḥsān. Sarakhsī's focus is that, so far as the qiyās is concerned, it should be analyzed and examined as to whether its 'illa is demonstrated in the process of reasoning to be connected with the aṣl (Origin) and when he deals with the doctrine of istiḥsān, he observes and maintains the same vigor of criteria. The difference lies only in the fact that when he deals with the doctrine of qiyās, Sarakhsī is generally addressing the religious affairs (aḥkām al-dīn), whereas with the doctrine of istiḥsān, he tries to deal with the aḥkām al-dunyā (worldly affairs), mu'āmalāt (mutual relations) of Muslims with other nations, muwāda'a (treatise) and furū' (branches of law).

Sarakhsī's works are investigated in this context and our main concern is to present the much-ignored contributions of Sarakhsī's works with regard to the development and systematization of his doctrine of juristic preference and, most importantly, in relation with the muwāda'a (treatise) which, properly speaking, falls under the worldly affairs (aḥkām al-dunyā). Although Sarakhsī's position in the history of Islamic jurisprudence is recognized, the real significance of his works as well as import of his doctrine of juristic preference and his treatment of the subject matter of muwāda'a and mu'āmalāt have not yet been taken into cognizance.

Sarakhsī's works are considered generally as the commentaries on Shaybānī's works and to that extent only as the exposition of his works. But, our present investigation leads us to a different conclusion. On the one hand, Sarakhsī systematizes the doctrine of juristic preference to its fullest and seeks its justification directly from the sharī'a sources (namely, the Qur'ān, Ḥadīth and ijmā') as one does in the qiyās (the doctrine of systematic reasoning). Sarakhsī clearly defines what was conceived of as the doctrine of juristic preference in a rudimentary form by Abū Ḥanīfa and Abū Yūsuf. On the other hand, Sarakhsī shows the relevance of the doctrine of juristic preference and its application to the muwāda'a (treaties), mu'āmalāt (mutual relations) of Muslims with other nations concerning the aḥkām al-dunyā (worldly affairs). Sarakhsī is the one who conceives of the siyar (Conduct) as being a systematic discipline by defining it as "that which describes the conduct of Muslims with the unbelievers of enemy territory as well as the ones who enjoy the promise of security from the Muslims (mustā'min) or the dhimmīs (inhabitants of the territory protected by a treaty of surrender) in the territory of Islam and with the apostates...and the rebels...."[10]

With this, Sarakhsī sets forth the siyar (Conduct) as an autonomous and legitimate discipline within the framework of sharī'a law and attempts to establish the relevance of the doctrine of juristic preference with the mutual relations (mu'āmalāt) of Muslims with other nations. According to Sarakhsī, in this case the 'illa to be employed in the doctrine of juristic preference is "convenience, facilitation and what is accommodating to the people".[11] This can be done, according to Sarakhsī, by employing the concept of tawassu' (extension)[12] in the doctrine of juristic preference, which enables him to broaden the scope of Islamic jurisprudence including the mu'āmalāt (mutual relations) of Muslims with other nations and muwāda'a (treaties) concerning the aḥkām al-dunyā (worldly affairs).

In his **Uṣūl al-Fiqh**, Sarakhsī deals with the principles of Islamic jurisprudence and the exercise of ra'y in the form of the doctrine of systematic reasoning (qiyās) and the doctrine of juristic preference (istiḥsān). In the **Mabsūṭ**, he develops and systematizes the doctrine of juristic preference and shows its relevance to the siyar (Conduct) and in the **Sharḥ al-Siyar al-Kabīr** demonstrates its application within the framework of sharī'a law. Here, we find the employment of public utterances and official instructions of the Caliphs which the jurists incorporated in the law and still other rules and practices evolving from the mutual reciprocity and commensurability with other nations. The Sunna and local practices are equivalent to the 'āda (customs); the Qur'ān and Ḥadīth, the Prophet's utterances and Caliph's decisions and instructions represent authority (āthār); the principles and rules enshrined in the treaties with other nations fall under the category of agreement ('ahd and muwāda'a) and the writings of the jurists helped to formulate the legal ordinances rather than the laws as Khaddhuri formulates,[13] since Isamic law is, strictly speaking, not a statute law. The legal ordinances were formulated by a rational method of interpretation (ra'y) and the religious standards and moral rules which were introduced into the legal subject matter provided the framework for its structural order[14] and may be said to represent the methodological reasoning (ra'y) in the form of the doctrine of systematic reasoning and the doctrine of juristic preference. The tendency of taking material facts into account, diverging from the formally correct decision for reasons such as fairness, appropriateness, reciprocity, necessity etc., is not unknown in Islamic jurisprudence. It appears in the doctrine of istiḥsān and the doctrine of istiṣlāḥ, but this principle, both in theory and in its actual application, occupies too subordinate a position for it to be able to have great impact on positive law. The importance of Sarakhsī's doctrine of juristic preference lies in positive law. The importance of Sarakhsī's doctrine of juristic preference lies in the fact that he develops it systematically by incorporating all the material facts and analyzes them methodologically enriching them into positive content of Islamic jurisprudence.[15] In his treatment of this subject matter, Sarakhsī employs various constitutive elements such as the 'illa in the doctrine of juristic preference which enable him to deal with the mutual relations (mu'āmalāt) of Muslims with other nations and muwāda'a (treaties). Khadduri has expounded on Shaybānī's siyar (Conduct) sufficiently, but has not investigated from the standpoint of the methodological reasoning (ra'y) in the form of the doctrine of qiyās and the doctrine of istiḥsān, which may be due to the fact that it was not his contention and moreover, Shaybānī's writings still represented the formative period of Islamic jurisprudence. It is in Sarakhsī's works that we find the treatment of the subject matter of siyar (Conduct) from the methodological standpoint especially in the form of the doctrine of istiḥsān to deal with the mutual relations of Muslims with other nations (mu'āmalāt) and treaties (muwāda'a) concerning the worldly affairs (aḥkām al-dunyā).

With this clarification regarding the use of ra'y in the form of the doctrine of qiyās (systematic reasoning) and the doctrine of istiḥsān (juristic preference), we shall now provide a brief overview of the nature of Sarakhsī's doctrine of juristic preference and explain how Sarakhsī develops and systematizes it.

Sarakhsī in his **Mabsūṭ** defines the doctrine of istiḥsān (juristic preference) as the abandonment of the opinion to which reasoning by the doctrine of qiyās (systematic reasoning) would lead, in favor of a different opinion supported by stronger evidence and adapted to what is accommodating to the people.[16] Thereby, Sarakhsī neither undermines the importance of the exercise of the doctrine of systematic reasoning nor rejects it in any sense. As a matter of fact, Sarakhsī uses it extensively and finds it quite appropriate in the aḥkām al-dīn (religious affairs) but, when it comes to the aḥkām al-dunyā (wordly affairs), mu'āmlāt (mutual relations) of Muslims with other nations, muwāda'a (treatise) and furū' (branches of law), Sarakhsī finds it necessary to extend it to the doctrine of juristic preference, but not without rigid and vigorous application according to the criteria and formal conditions laid down for the exercise of ra'y (reasoning) in any form. As in the doctrine of systematic reasoning, the 'illa (effective reasoning) should be based on and connected with the aṣl (Origin), so is the case in the exercise and application of juristic preference. Sarakhsī's contribution lies in showing and demonstrating how and on what grounds facilitation, comfort, necessity and other neighboring concepts which enter into the subject matter of muwāda'a (treaties) such as appropriateness, reciprocity and other formal considerations can be used as the 'illa in the doctrine of juristic preference to justify and validate it.

In order to develop and systematize the doctrine of juristic preference, Sarakhsī employs the following main concepts which are explained here briefly:

(i) The ta'līl (inference) is initially defined as the inference of a judgment (ḥukm) based on the 'illa (effective reasoning). Sarakhsī analyzes this concept mainly to show that the 'illa used in the doctrine of juristic preference is strong, although not apparent.

(ii) The tarjīḥ (preference) of a judgment as against the other, such as preferred qiyās; namely, the qiyās which is supported by the istiḥsān on certain grounds which emerge in Sarakhsī's analysis as the tarjīḥ (preference).

iii) The wujh al-iḥtijāj (ground of what is binding); namely, when the various kinds of reasonings are included under the qiyās, but they differ from one another in antecedence of the qiyās of either one of them or its source or the source of both or the circumstance, that one is more clear than the other. This clarity becomes the ground (wujh) to view it as the justification to use it in the doctrine of istiḥsān.

In Sarakhsī's analysis of the doctrine of istiḥsān (juristic preference) in all these various aspects, one discerns the use of the essential notion of ma'ānī (inward meaning) for the basis and justification of the doctrine of istiḥsān (juristic preference), as we would see it in the course of our investigation.

Lastly, the most important aspect of Sarakhsī's thought needs to be emphasized. Sarakshsī employs the doctrine of istiḥsān (juristic preference) mainly dealing with the contents of muwāda'a (treaties), mu'āmalāt (mutual relations) concerning the aḥkām al-dunyā (worldly affairs) and subjects them intensely to vigorous analysis in juxtaposition with the doctrine of istiḥsān (juristic preference) by taking into consideration the material facts, such as, dhimma (protection), amān (peace agreement), tabāyun al-dārayn (disparity of territories) and other factors such as, the questions regarding the reciprocity (mujāzā), necessity (ḍarūra) and customs (ʻādāt) and shows how the siyar (Conduct) can become an autonomous discipline and widen the scope of Islamic jurisprudence within the framework of sharīʻa law.

The gist of our present investigation is to examine Sarakhsī's contentions from and on the basis of his works and come to the conclusion so that it can become significant and related to the modern day Muslim world.

A glossary of frequently used terms, designed as a quick reference for the reader, can be found at the end of the book.

CHAPTER ONE

Sarakhsī's Biographical Account, His Stature and Contributions in Islamic Jurisprudence

SARAKHSĪ: THE MAN AND HIS WORKS:

Muḥammad bin Aḥmad Abū Bakr Shams ul-Imām Sarakhsī belonged to the place S-R-khs,[1] pronounced "s" as "sa", "r" as "ra" and "kh" pronounced without a vowel. It is the ancient city of Khorāsān. It is called Sarakhs after the name of a person who built it.[2] Sam'ānī mentions that it was restored by Dhūl Qarnayn.[3] Nothing is known of Sarakhsī's early childhood, his family background or its origin. It is also not certain exactly which year he was born; hence it would be impossible to ascertain the span of his lifetime. Discrepant accounts are given of the year of his death. It is said that Sarakhsī died in the year 483 A.H./1090 A.D.

Quṭlūbugha, one of the oldest sources, maintains that Sarakhsī died around 500 A.H./ 1106 A.D.,[4] while Khalīfa[5] and Laknawī[6] agree that Sarakhsī died around 483 A.H./1090 A.D. This seems probable as we know through various accounts that Ḥuṣayrī,[7] one of his students who took dictation from Sarakhsī in the prison and committed it to writing, died in the year 500 A.H./1106 A.D., which suggests that Sarakhsī's death should have occurred earlier. A very strong impression is given by Laknawī[8] that Sarakhsī died right after finishing his dictation of **Sharḥ al-Siyar al-Kabīr** and that means, if Ḥuṣayrī took dictation, then Sarakhsi's death should have occurred earlier than 500 A.H./1106 A.D.

SARAKHSĪ'S SOLITARY CONFINEMENT:

It is said that Sarakhsī was held in solitary confinement because of his advice to the ruler of the time with regard to a juristic matter. It is narrated by Ibn Quṭlūbughā that Amīr married the slave woman belonging to one of his servants during her waiting period. He sought advice from the scholars of the time with regard to the validity of this marriage and they responded by replying: "it is best what you did." Sarakhsī was the only one to declare it to be invalid, because a slave woman becomes free in this case and marrying her is considered as if she were a free woman. Hence, the waiting period becomes incumbent on her after the emancipation.[9] As a consequence, Sarakhsī was thrown into the prison in the year 466 A.H./1073 A.D.,[10] where he spent more than fifteen years and dictated to the students his most important works, the **Mabsūṭ**, the **Uṣūl** and the **Sharḥ al-Siyar al-Kabīr,** entirely from memory without having any reading material at hand. Parts of his **Mabsūṭ** are dated from the prison in the years 466 A.H./1084 A.D. When Sarakhsī reached the fourth part of his **Sharḥ al-Siyar al-Kabīr**, he was released from the prison. He completed it in the court of Amīr Ḥasan in Marghīnān in Jamādā al-ūlā in the year 480 A.H./1090 A.D.[11]

It is also interesting to note that all biographers of Sarakhsī show a great admiration for his memory as one can see from the Appendix, where the translations of various accounts of Sarakhsī's life and his works are provided. It is said that Shāfi'ī (204 A.H./820 A.D.) committed three hundred quires, while it is believed that Sarakhsī had committed one thousand and three hundred complete quires to memory.[12] In those days, great importance was given to the memory; but with this, one should not ignore the fact that some of the traditions (aḥādīth) Sarakhsī narrates are not in the same wordings as found in the sources. This may be due to the fact that he was in the prison during the time when he dictated his **Sharḥ al-Siyar al-Kabīr**, but when he came out of prison and wrote the last part of it, we find that Sarakhsī's accounts from Wāqidī's **al-Maghāzī** are almost exact.[13]

SARAKHSĪ'S WORKS:

Sarakhsī was a prolific writer. His best known works include the **Sharḥ al-Siyaral-Kabīr** (Hyderabad edition 4 Volumes, Cairo edition, 5 Volumes) and **Mabsūṭ** (30 Volumes), which are generally considered as commentaries and explanations on Shaybānī's works. One of Sarakhsī's most important works is the **Uṣūl al-Fiqh** (2 Volumes) to which not enough attention has been paid. In this work, Sarakhsī discusses at great length the traditional sources of Islamic jurisprudence and emphasizes the import and significance of the doctrine of juristic preference.

Other lesser known works mentioned in various sources include **al-Nukat** which is the **Sharḥ** of Shaybānī's **Ziyāda al-Ziyādāt**.[14] Schacht mentions that in some sources **the Kitāb al-Makhārij fī a-Ḥayal** is attributed to Sarakhsī.[15] It is also indicated by Schacht that the **Mabsūṭ** attributed by Abū Ḥafs to Sarakhsī is a commentary on the Epitome of (Shaybānī's) **Kitāb al-Aṣl** and **al-Kāfī** by Muḥammad ibn Muḥammad ibn Aḥmad al-Marawazī al-Ḥakim al-Shahīd.[16] Khalīfa attributes also the **Fawā'id** and **Kitāb al-Ḥaiḍ** to Sarakhsī.[17] The latter is obviously a part of the **Mabsūṭ** and **Sharḥ al-Siyar al-Kabīr**. Quṭlūbughā also attributes the Sharḥ al-Ṭahāwī to him.[18] Finally, Khaṣṣāf's **Ādāb al-Qādī** is mentioned as being written by Sarakhsī.[19]

THE NATURE AND CHARACTERISTICS OF SARAKHSĪ'S WORKS:

Sarakhsī's **Uṣūl al-Fiqh** and **Mabsūṭ** are relatively precise in diction and at times, especially in the **Uṣūl al-Fiqh**, Sarakhsī is very eloquent. In many parts of the **Sharḥ al-Siyar al-Kabīr**, one can notice the poor diction, long sentences and negligence in their grammatical structure. Munajjid maintains that this is due to the fact that later scholars of Islamic jurisprudence did not concern themselves as much with language and diction as did earlier scholars and also because Sarakhsī dictated most parts of his **Sharḥ** while he was in the prison in Transoxiana and did not revise it.[20] It would be more appropriate to say that the latter is the case.

CHAPTER TWO

Development of the Doctrine of Juristic Preference In Sarakhsī's Works and its Significance regarding Worldly Affairs

Section I: SARAKHSĪ AND THE HISTORICAL DEVELOPMENT OF SYSTEMATIC REASONING (QIYĀS) AND THE DOCTRINE OF JURISTIC PREFERENCE (ISTIḤSĀN)

Generally speaking, the doctrine of qiyās (systematic reasoning) came to be recognized as one of the valid sources for the derivation of laws in the early development of Islamic jurisprudence, although not without dispute. As already mentioned in the Introduction, in the beginning, the controversy took place between the traditionalists (ahl al-ḥadīth) and the rationalists (ahl al-ra'y),[1] but gradually the doctrine of qiyās (systematic reasoning) and later the doctrine of istiḥsān (juristic preference) paved the way in the Ḥanafī school of thought in the form of ra'y (individual opinion).

The earliest employment of the term "istiḥsān" is associated with Abū Ḥanīfa (150 A.H./767 A.D.), who uses it synonymously with and in the sense of the "ra'y" (individual opinion).[2] Initially, it was subsumed by Abū Ḥanīfa under the qiyās (doctrine of systematic reasoning) without maintaining any distinction between the two doctrines as began with Abū Yūsuf (182 A.H./798 A.D.) and Shaybānī (189 A.H./804 A.D.). Nor does he clarify the basis for its validity in Islamic jurisprudence. Abū Yūsuf, following Abū Ḥanīfa, introduces a refinement of the term with explicit reference to the tradition (Ḥadīth). Abū Yūsuf refutes Abū Ḥanīfa's crude doctrine of systematic reasoning and anticipates in essentials Shāfi'ī's relevant objections regarding the validity of the doctrine of juristic preference.[3]

Abū Yūsuf uses the term istīḥsān in his **Kitāb al-Kharāj** in four places,[4] but notyet in a technical sense. It is understood by Abū Yūsuf as the qiyās, without any explanation as to how the istiḥsān is different from the qiyās in its 'illa (effective reasoning) and on what grounds the qiyās can be extended to the istiḥsān. This becomes clear when we discuss all four instances in which Abū Yūsuf employs the term.

The first instance is regarding the punishment by divine laws (ḥudūd allāh) of a sin. If someone commits a sin with a slave woman and then buys her, the punishment by devine law becomes incumbent on him (by the doctrine of systematic reasoning) and if he has committed sin and thereafter kills her, it is better (istaḥsana) that he pay the price for her and there is no punishment executed by divine law.[5] The legal implication here is the consideration and ease in punishment in contrast to the severe punishment as ruled by the doctrine of systematic reasoning in the case of a free (Muslim) woman. Abū Yūsuf deviates here from the doctrine of systematic reasoning, but fails to provide any reasoning in order to deduce such an inference. The second instance involves the cases of stealing, intoxication and fornication. If the Imām finds anyone committing such acts, then by the doctrine of systematic reasoning, it is necessary for the Imām to execute the punishment by divine law, but the istiḥsān (juristic preference) lies in that it becomes established only by evidence and this is according to what has reached us from the authorities (āthār).[6] The third instance is regarding anyone who is accused of false testimony or fornication or anyone who is accused of stealing and his hands are to be cut off as the punishment by divine law. In this case, it is better (istaḥsana) that we hear the evidence.[7] We adhere to the divine law until the evidence is established. In both of these instances the consideration is the severity of the punishment: the more severe the punishment, the more certainty of evidence is required so that no doubt is left in the validity of the execution of punishment. But, Abū Yūsuf does not give any ground or explanation which can provide explicit 'illa (effective reasoning) on the basis of aṣl (Origin), thus lacking the validity required for the systematic use of the doctrine of juristic preference. Last instance is regarding the case of mustā'min (person who enjoys the promise of security from Muslims) who comes to the territory of Islam and is found stealing the property of a Muslim. According to the doctrine of systematic reasoning, it is valid for the Muslim to cut his hands off. Abū Yūsuf declares it is better (istaḥsana) not to agree with the one who holds this opinion,[8] but again without giving any explanation.

From analyzing these instances, one can see that Abū Yūsuf uses the notion of istiḥsān but fails to provide any ground for deviating from the doctrine of systematic reasoning as to how its 'illa is constituted and derived from the aṣl (Origin), and in what way does it differ from the usual 'illa of the doctrine of systematic reasoning. In short, Abū Yūsuf employs the notion of istiḥsān vaguely and is not clear as to the nature of its distinct 'illa and how the istiḥsān is based on it.

In **Jāmi' al-Ṣaghīr**, as found on the margin of Abū Yūsuf's **Kitāb al-Kharāj**, Shaybānī anticipates Shāfi'ī by giving a strict interpretation of the doctrine of systematic reasoning[9] based on the tradition (ḥadīth), but still using ra'y (personal discretion) to the extent used in the Antiquity.[10] In Shaybānī's **Jāmi' al-Ṣaghīr**, there is no discussion on the doctrine of istiḥsān and on what grounds it can be considered as validly based on the aṣl (Origin). Shaybānī neither expounds on the doctrine of istiḥsān nor makes any systematic use of the doctrine by basing it on the concept of 'illa as does Sarakhsī in his works. From this it can be concluded that it is very unlikely that Sarakhsī could have borrowed from Shaybānī the concept of juristic preference and its employment in the subject matter of muwāda'a (treaties) and mu'āmalāt (mutual relations) concerning the aḥkām al-dunyā (worldly affairs).

Section II: SARAKHSĪ'S DOCTRINE OF JURISTIC PREFERENCE AND THE CONCEPT OF TREATIES AS DEVELOPED IN HIS **MABSŪṬ** AND **BĀB AL-MUWĀDA'A**

Generally, scholars of Islamic jurisprudence maintain that Sarakhsī (483 A.H./1090 A.D.) was a follower of Shaybānī (189 A.H./804 A.D.) and, at most, an expounder and commentator of his works, although his stature is raised by some next to those who are in the ranks of associates of Abū Ḥanīfa.[11] It is said that he reached the stature of Abū Bakr al-Khaṣṣāf (291 A.H./903 A.D.), Abū Ḥasan al-Karkhī (340 A.H./951 A.D.), al-Pazdawī (482 A.H./1089 A.D.), and others.[12] However, such statements are not based on any systematic analysis of his works. It becomes evident from our present investigation that Sarakhsī, in fact, derives his material from all these sources, including Abū Yūsuf whom Shaybānī does not like to refer to in his works because of the enmity which took place between them[13] and Shāfi'ī who launched a great rebuttal against the upholders of the doctrine of juristic preference. Sarakhsī is not concerned with such trivial matters. He states the opinion of Abū Yūsuf whenever he finds it necessary and brings it in support of his opinion when it differs from the opinion of Shaybānī;[14] and, inspite of Shāfi'ī's opposition to the doctrine of juristic preference, Sarakhsī occasionally cites and accepts his opinion in order to support his own opinion against Shaybānī or others.[15] Sarakhsī's main concern is how to deal with the contents of muwāda'a (treaties) and mu'āmalāt (mutual relations) from the point of view of juristic preference within the framework of and on the basis of sharī'a law and provide a formal unity to their subject matter.

As a matter of fact, the main theme of Sarakhsī's **Bāb al-Muwāda'a** of **Sharḥ al-Siyar al-Kabīr** is to establish the formal structure of muwāda'a (treaties) and incorporate the subject matter of mu'āmalāt within the framework of sharī'a law and expound it from the point of view of the doctrine of juristic preference. In the course of our investigation, we shall focus on these main features as they emerge by analyzing Sarakhsī's works. It is appropriate at this point to clarify that Sarakhsī in his **Mabsūṭ** follows Shaybānī based on the fact that we find parallels with the ordering of chapters and themes as discussed by Shaybānī in his **Jāmi' al-Ṣaghīr** and **Kitāb al-Aṣl**, but with a very important difference: the chapter on the doctrine of juristic preference in their works is to be found in a different context. In Shaybānī's **Kitāb al-Aṣl**, the chapter on the doctrine of juristic preference is followed by the discussions regarding the laws dealing with the religious affairs (aḥkām al-dīn),[16] while in Sarakhsī's **Mabsūṭ**, in contrast to and in anticipation of what has already been laid down in his **Uṣūl al-Fiqh**, we find the discussions followed not only by the laws related to the religious affairs, but also by the laws related to the worldly affairs (aḥkām al-dunyā), such as the laws regarding the unbelievers, dhimmīs (the inhabitants of the territory protected by the treaty of surrender), mustā'mins (those who enjoy the promise of security from Muslims), apostates, rebels etc.[17] In his earlier work, **Uṣūl al-Fiqh**, Sarakhsī has not initially brought out the concept of treaties as an autonomous discipline and in juxtaposition with the doctrine of juristic preference. In his **Mabsūṭ**, Sarakhsī gradually develops the concept of his doctrine of juristic preference and directly brings out his views on the matters of muwāda'a (treaties) and mu'āmalāt (mutual relations) according to it, pointing out the differences from what is being maintained by the jurists according to the doctrine of systematic reasoning; and finally, in his **Bāb al-muwāda'a,** Sarakhsī analyzes the muwāda'a (treaties) and mu'āmalāt (mutual relations) making it explicit how the doctrine of juristic preference is extended and used by showing that its 'illa is derived from the aṣl (Origin). From this and especially when one considers that Shaybānī's **al-Siyar al-Kabīr** is lost,[18] it may be concluded that Sarakhsī in his works employs the doctrine of juristic preference mainly for the purpose of muwāda'a (treaties) and mu'āmalāt (mutual relations) on the basis of its 'illa, which is different from the usual 'illa employed in the doctrine of systematic reasoning.

Section III: BASIS AND JUSTIFICATION OF SARAKHSĪ'S CONCEPT OF MUWĀDA'A (TREATIES)

In his **Mabsūṭ**, Sarakhsī makes it very explicit that the muwāda'a deals solely with the matters concerning the mutual relations (mu'āmalāt) between Muslims and other nations,[19] but it is to be justified on the basis of sharī'a law and conducted within its framework. These other nations, according to Sarakhsī, are the unbelievers from the enemy territory, dhimmīs, mustā'mins, apostates, rebels, Jews and Christians.[20]

In his **Bāb al-Muwāda'a**, Sarakhsī focuses on the basis of such a concept of muwāda'a and asserts that the perspective of the mutual relations between Muslims and other nations, such as the matters of amān (promise of security), dhimma (protection) etc., is of a broader nature and more facilitating.[21] Thus, in order to establish such a concept of autonomous discipline of muwāda'a, Sarakhsī makes a clear and categorical distinction between the religious affairs (aḥkām al-dīn) which, strictly speaking, are concerns only of the Muslims and the wordly affairs (aḥkām al-dunyā)[22] which are the sole concerns not only of Muslims, but of other nations as well. The muwāda'a deals with and belongs to the worldly affairs. By its very nature, muwāda'a demands flexibility and to be treated on that accord. The religious affairs are, strictly speaking, meant for those who are Muslims wherein the strict enforcement of the laws becomes obligatory, whereas the muwāda'a is pursued with a wider perspective in mind and, therefore, needs to be conducted with flexibility. This is achieved by what Sarakhsī calls the tawassu',[23] which literally means extension. Sarakhsī is consistent in bringing out this concept both implicitly and explicitly in his works as well as stating it as a premise for the establishment of muwāda'a as an autonomous discipline. Since the nature of worldly affairs has a broader perspective, it needs to be conducted by extending the doctrine of systematic reasoning and thus, according to Sarakhsī, the need for the employment of the doctrine of juristic preference in the subject matter of muwāda'a (treaties) and mu'āmalāt (mutual relations). Nonetheless, the basis of such a doctrine should be found within the framework of sharī'a law as is the case with the doctrine of systematic reasoning. Although Sarakhsī initially considers in his **Uṣūl al-Fiqh** the doctrine of juristic preference as a kind of reasoning and as such not different from the doctrine of systematic reasoning, in his **Mabsūṭ** and **Bāb al-Muwāda'a**, Sarakhsī strives to find the basis of the doctrine of juristic preference not in the doctrine of systematic reasoning, but in the aṣl (Origin) itself, namely the Qur'ān, Ḥadīth and ijmā'. Thus, as we shall see later, Sarakhsī sets forth the argument for the justification and validity of the doctrine of juristic preference.

Section IV: NATURE OF THE TREATIES (MUWĀDA'A) AND ITS INCORPORATION WITHIN THE FRAMEWORK OF SHARĪ'A LAW

In chapters I, II, and V of **Bab al-Muwāda'a** of **Sharḥ al-Sayir al-Kabīr**, Sarakhsī discusses the nature of muwāda'a as being the legal contract between two parties the main purpose of which is to facilitate and maintain the mutual relations between them. The treaty should be signed by both parties stating specifically all the stipulations to be observed and executed during a specific time period before it is signed and sealed. It is conceived in the nature of a binding contract for both parties. Thus, Sarakhsī provides its formal unity and its legal structure and arrangement from the superstructure of the sharī'a law as it emerges from the Qur'ān and Ḥadīth.[24] In essence, the legal structure of muwāda'a is incorporated into the sharī'a law. Here, Sarakhsī shows how to extend and incorporate the muwāda'a formally into sharī'a law by the doctrine of juristic preference, as such matters fall only within the scope of the doctrine of juristic preference, since the muwāda'a is wider in its perspective and deals with other nations in worldly affairs rather than only in religious affairs. Hence, by necessity, we have to extend the doctrine of systematic reasoning by the doctrine of juristic preference. Sarakhsī does so in this case with the concept of stipulations (shurūṭ) of the treaty.

Kruse gives an example of it from Sarakhsī's **Bāb al-Muwāda'a**, but does not relate it to the differences in reasoning involved in the doctrine of systematic reasoning and the doctrine of juristic preference:

> The preposition 'alā (on, against) indicates the stipulation for a certain condition. When e.g. the muwāda'a is entered into for the period of three years 'alā 3,000 dinars, it is a proof that the fulfillment of muwāda'a is the condition for the payment of the tribute agreed upon. There is full accord between the wordings of the treaty and the actual nature of muwāda'a so that in this case nothing would justify a deviation from the rules for the dissolution of a treaty as laid down by istiḥsān (doctrine of juristic preference). On the other hand, however, the proposition bi (with) denotes that a consideration has been agreed upon. The conclusion of a muwāda'a for the period of three years by 100 dinars for every year would mean that in this case, the tribute is explicitly intended to be a consideration. The muwāda'a is a barter contract on the strength of explicit agreement. It can be treated unhesitatingly in analogy to a lease.[25]

Kruse emphasizes the secondary nature of muwāda'a when it is considered as a treaty and when it is treated as a barter contract. This is, no doubt, an important point in the matters of muwāda'a, but more significant is the difference in the doctrinal approach. The former case is dealt with according to the doctrine of juristic preference and the latter according to the doctrine of systematic reasoning. What Sarakhsī shows is that in the matters of muwāda'a (treaties) and mu'āmalāt (mutual relations), the emphasis lies on the fulfillment of a treaty and facilitation of the mutual relations between the two nations and its basis should be widened and can only be dealt with by the doctrine of juristic preference rather than the doctrine of systematic reasoning. What emerges from the treatment of this theme is that the basis of muwāda'a lies in the doctrine of juristic preference since such matters, by their very nature, are broader and wider in scope which forces us to extend them on a different 'illa not provided in the doctrine of systematic reasoning.

CHAPTER THREE

Effective Reasoning of the Doctrine of Juristic Preference and Justification for its Employment in Treaties and Mutual Relations

Section I: BASIS OF 'ILLA (EFFECTIVE REASONING) OF THE DOCTRINE OF JURISTIC PREFERENCE IN THE AṢL (ORIGIN)

Sarakhsī in his **Mabsūṭ** defines the doctrine of istiḥsān (juristic preference) as the abandonment of the opinion to which reasoning by the doctrine of qiyās (systematic reasoning) would lead, in favor of a different opinion supported by stronger evidence and adapted to what is accommodating to the people.[1] Sarakhsī definitely argues for the use of the doctrine of juristic preference only in this sense and seeks support for it directly from the Qur'ān and Ḥadīth. Thus, according to Sarakhsī, such a deviation from the doctrine of systematic reasoning is only to be based on the evidence found in the Qur'ān and Ḥadīth. In anticipation of his **Bāb al-Muwāda'a,** we find that Sarakhsī argues for the doctrine of juristic preference on the basis of an 'illa which is different in nature and justified on different grounds than the 'illa which is usually employed in the doctrine of systematic reasoning. That is to say, the 'illa to be used in the doctrine of juristic preference is from a different perspective due to the fact that Islamic jurisprudence, as seen in its historical development, is not statute law but takes into account the material facts and incorporates them, especially in the matters of muwāda'a (treaties) and mu'āmalāt (mutual relations) concerning the aḥkām al-dunyā (worldly affairs), and thereby, its scope is widened and enriched.

According to Sarakhsī, the 'illa employed in the doctrine of juristic preference is convenience, facilitation and what is accommodating to the people. It strives and seeks for equanimity and flexibility. As a result, the hardship is left behind.[2] Sarakhsī provides the evidence for the 'illa (effective reasoning) of the doctrine of juristic preference first from the Qur'ān and then from the Ḥadīth (tradition). From the Qur'ān, he cites, "God intends every facility for you and not hardship,"[3] and narrates the following tradition: "it is better that there is an ease in your religion."[4] Thus, Sarakhsī seeks support for the basis and the justification of the doctrine directly from the Qur'ān and Ḥadīth.

Section II: 'ILLA (EFFECTIVE REASONING) AS THE BASIS FOR THE DIFFERENCES BETWEEN THE SYSTEMATIC REASONING AND THE DOCTRINE OF JURISTIC PREFERENCE

In his **Uṣūl al-Fiqh**, Sarakhsī, while discussing the nature of 'illa as employed in the doctrine of systematic reasoning and the doctrine of juristic preference, subsumes both of them under the general category of ijtihād (exercise of legal reasoning) and brings out support for the use of qiyās (systematic reasoning) and ra'y (individual opinion) or what he later calls the istiḥsān (juristic preference in the technical sense) from several traditions. For instance, when the Prophet sent Mu'ādh as the Qadi to Yemen, he asked: "how would you adjudicate?" Mu'ādh replied: "by the book of God." The Prophet asked him further: "if you do not find any guidance in the book of God, what will you do?" Mu'ādh replied: "by the Sunna of the Prophet." Thereupon, the Prophet asked him, "if you do not find it in the Sunna, then what will you do?" Mu'ādh replied: "I shall exercise my own individual opinion (ijtahdu ra'y)."[5] Thus, when there are no precedents set forth in the Qur'ān or Sunna, the exercise of individual opinion is allowed. In the section on the Qiyās and Istiḥsān of his **Uṣul al-Fiqh**,[6] Sarakhsī argues for the validity of the doctrine of systematic reasoning (qiyās) on the basis of its 'illa (effective reasoning) as being ẓāhir (apparent),[7] but raises a further point in terms of its being qawī (strong) or ḍaī'f (weak). The effective reasoning employed in the doctrine of systematic reasoning may be apparent but not necessarily strong. When such is the case, Sarakhsī argues for the exercise of individual opinion or what he later terms as the istiḥsān on the ground of the strength of the 'illa (effective reasoning) to be used and concludes that the abandonment is allowed in favor of the istiḥsān, when the stronger evidence (athar) is found.[8]

In the **Mabsūṭ**, Sarakhsī asserts that the istiḥsān (juristic preference) is a kind of qiyas (systematic reasoning) and both are, in fact, not different from each other except that the 'illa (effective reasoning) employed in both of them is of a different nature. In the doctrine of systematic reasoning, it is apparent (jalīy) but weak (ḍa'īf) in its evidence (athar) and in the doctrine of juristic preference, the 'illa used is concealed (khafī) but strong (qawī) in its evidence.[9] From this point on, Sarakhsi goes further and tries to establish that such a nature of 'illa of the doctrine of juristic preference consists in and is founded on the notion of comfort, ease, equanimity and what is accommodating to the people.[10] Thus, when neessary, the 'illa which is strong although concealed should be employed and when used in the doctrine of juristic preference, it has a stronger ground and a firmer footing than the usual 'illa which is explicit or apparent but weak as used in the doctrine of systematic reasoning; and, therefore, the 'illa of the doctrine of juristic preference should take precedence. Sarakhsī makes it clear, by giving an example, that "this world" is to be considered as an 'illa which is apparent but the "other world" is to be considered as an 'illa which is concealed in the sense of purity and perfection.[11] Thus, when this implicit or concealed 'illa is used in the doctrine of juristic preference, it should be considered stronger and employed therewith. To conclude, the doctrine of systematic reasoning and juristic preference both are similar in this respect that they both are based on the concept of 'illa (effective reasoning), but are different in the nature of the 'illa they employ.

Section III: SARAKHSĪ'S DEFENSE AGAINST SHĀFI'Ī'S REBUTTAL OF THE DOCTRINE OF JURISTIC PREFERENCE ON THE BASIS OF THE CONCEPT OF EFFECTIVE REASONING AND THE CONDITIONS FOR ITS VALIDITY

As already known in the history of Islamic jurisprudence, Shāfi'ī was the greatest opponent of the ra'y (exercise of individiual opinion) in general and the doctrine of juristic preference (istiḥsān) in particular. In his **Uṣūl al-Fiqh,** while discussing the nature of the doctrine of systematic reasoning and the doctrine of juristic preference, Sarakhsī deals with the objections raised by Shāfi'ī in the **Ibṭāl al-Istiḥsān** (Rebuttal of the Doctrine of Juristic Preference) of his **Kitāb al-Umm**[12] and **Risāla**[13] and shows by analyzing that the istiḥsān, contrary to what Shāfi'ī maintains, is based on the 'illa or what Shāfi'ī names as the khabar (narrative be it the text of the Qur'ān or Sunna).[14] Perhaps this is one of the reasons Sarakhsī asserts that the doctrine of juristic preference is, in fact, a kind of qiyās. According to Shāfi'ī, "they differ from one another in the antecedence of the analogy (qiyās) of either one of them, or its source or the source of both, or the circumstance that one is more clear than the other."[15] Sarakhsī analyzes all these aspects at great length in his **Uṣūl al-Fiqh** and shows that what Shāfi'ī brings out as objections are really no objections.[16] Shāfi'ī maintains that "no one (other than the Prophet) is allowed to make a decision except by istidlāl. . . . Nor should anyone make use of the istiḥsān (juristic preference), for to decide by the istiḥsān means initiating something himself without basing the decision upon a parallel example."[17] It is not permissible for everyone to exercise the isthsān, for only the scholars (fuqahā') -not others- may give an opinion and:

> the scholars hold that a narrative (whether it is a text of the Qur'ān or Sunna) must be followed. If a narrative is not to be found, analogy might be applied on the strength of a narrative, for if analogy were abandoned, it would be permissible for any intelligent man, other than the scholars, to exercise istiḥsān in the absence of a narrative.[18]
>
> If the jurist were to give an opinion (ra'y) based neither on a binding narrative nor an analogy, he is more liable to commit a sin than an ignorant person, if it were permissible for the latter to give an opinion. No one is permitted (after the death of the Prophet) to give an opinion except on the strength of the knowledge of the Qur'ān, Sunna and general consensus, narrative and analogy based upon these (texts). . . .[19]

Shāfi'ī objects against the use of the istiḥsān (juristic preference) and pronounces its complete rejection on the very basis on which the upholders of the doctrine of juristic preference maintain its justification, as he maintains that it is not valid for the jurists to adjudicate by exercising istiḥsān;[20] for it is solely to be done on the basis of textual support and the istiḥsān is to be considered as not being included in it. It is in order to deal with this issue systematically Sarakhsī first establishes in his **Mabsūṭ** that the 'illa of the doctrine of istiḥsān (juristic preference) is based on and derived from the Qur'ān and Ḥadīth; and, second, in order to do away with all the objections which were later raised in a very developed form from the Shāfi'ī and Mālikī schools of thought, Sarakhsī in his **Uṣūl al-Fiqh** explains that the principle, circumstances or necessity (ḍarūra) or for that matter any other material facts involved in any decision whether exercised by the ra'y in the form of the doctrine of qiyās or the doctrine of istiḥsān, are already accompanied in the command itself and provided in the Qur'ān or Sunna and are already inclusive with it,[21] especially in the matters of prayers and the religious sanctions ('ibādāt). Thus, here the 'illa, whether based on circumstance, necessity or any other material facts, already includes them as the constitutive elements of it and on the basis of which the 'illa is referred to what God has ordained and what his Prophet has said and the difference of opinion takes place as to whether the textual interpretation of it is based on the Qur'ān or Sunna. Naturally, the condition or the circumtance in which the difference of opinion arises in relation to the command or the sharī'a law is itself already inclusive in the exercise of qiyās.[22]

Sarakhsī makes this point more explicit when he discusses the validity of ijmā' (general consensus) as opposed to ra'y (individual opinion). Sarakhsī argues, it is generally maintained that whenever general consensus exists, it is sufficient and there is no further need for any exercise of opinion (ra'y), be it in the form of qiyās or istiḥsān, as the former implies certainty whereas the latter does not.[23] Sarakhsī defends the ra'y (in the form of the doctrine of qiyās and the doctrine of istiḥsān) on the basis of the 'illa and asserts that the claim, "the general consensus is certain, whereas the ra'y (qiyās or istiḥsān) is not," is merely a claim without any evidence. There is no evidence found against the ra'y (qiyās or istiḥsān) in the book of God,[24] as the establishment of it is found in consideration with the ma'ānī (inward meaning) based on the textual interpretation. The question of certainty is meaningless. It is rather the evidence or the binding proof of 'illa, whether employed in the ijmā' (general consensus) or the ra'y (individual opinion) in the form of the doctrine of qiyās and the doctrine of istiḥsān which is at the heart of the matter and the interpretation of it is determined by the ma'ānī (inward meaning) rather than the ṣūra (external form), even if it does not provide the certainty, such as one finds in the cases of traveling for the purpose of business or fighting against the enemy, but such things are not matters of knowledge with certainty. With this, it becomes evident that any kind of qiyās is based on the binding proof from the aṣl (Origin) and derives laws based on the 'illa (effective reasoning). In short, Sarakhsī shows here that the 'illa (effective reasoning) of juristic preference is a more viable basis and ground for its employment in the ra'y (individual opinion) in the form of the doctrine of qiyās (systematic reasoning) rather than simply the certainty which is provided in the ijmā' (general consensus). According to Sarakhsi, the same can be applied for the validity and justification of the doctrine of istiḥsān (juristic preference), since it is a kind of qiyās, or to put it in other words, an extension of the qiyās and the sole ground of the 'illa of the doctrine of juristic preference lies in and is constituted of material facts such as facilitation, laxity, ease and comfort. Thus, Sarakhsī quite successfully clears the way against Shāfi'ī's position, since once it becomes established that the 'illa (effective reasoning) employed in the doctrine of juristic preference is based on the evidence from the aṣl (Origin) it is in no case to be considered as being arbitrary, contrary to what Shāfi'ī maintains against the doctrine of juristic preference.

Additionally, the following conditions are necessary for the validity of the doctrine of systematic reasoning, which are equally to be observed and applied in the exercise of the doctrine of juristic preference. The first four conditions are specified by Sarakhsī in his **Uṣūl al-Fiqh**[25] and the last one in his **Bāb al-Muwāda'a**:[26]

(i) That the decision (ḥukm) reached by the aṣl (Origin), namely, the Qur'ān and the Sunna, is not determined on any other naṣṣ (textual evidence), namely, the ijmā' or qiyās.

(ii) That the 'illa (effective reasoning) employed in any kind of qiyās is not established in the same measure that its 'illa can be used to transcend the aṣl (Origin) in any circumstance or condition, for the aṣl (Origin) remains always the main criteria to determine any 'illa by which one arrives at the qiyās and, hence, its 'illa cannot be used to determine or transcend the aṣl (Origin) itself.

(iii) That after the use of 'illa (effective reasoning) employed in the doctrine of the qiyās (systematic reasoning), the laws based on textual interpretation remain the same as they were before.

(iv) That the 'illa (effective reasoning) is not applied to the wordings of the Text (the Qur'ān or Sunna), as the Text itself remains prior in its wordings and meanings.

(v) There is no further deduction of systematic reasoning from the previous one, but it should be based on and derived from the aṣl (Origin). In other words, the 'illa (effective reasoning) of any kind of doctrine of qiyās (systematic reasoning) can under no circumstances take the place of the aṣl (Origin) itself and become the basis for further deduction of systematic reasoning.

Section IV: CONSTITUTIVE ELEMENTS OF TREATIES (MUWĀDA'A) AS THE 'ILLA (EFFECTIVE REASONING) FOR THE EMPLOYMENT OF THE DOCTRINE OF JURISTIC PREFERENCE

Discussions with regard to the doctrine of systematic reasoning and the doctrine of juristic preference are generally found in the history of Islamic jurisprudence for the purpose of broadening the scope of Islamic jurisprudence and, in general, all the Ḥanafī jurists make use of the doctrine of juristic preference in the aḥkām al-dīn (religious affairs) as well as the aḥkām al-dunyā (worldly affairs), but for Sarakhsī its relevance and import lies more in the worldly affairs related with the matters of mu'āmalāt (mutual relations) and muwāda'a (treaties) due to the fact that they are broader and wider in their nature and concern not only Muslims but other nations as well and, therefore, other kinds of material facts enter into consideration. Sarakhsī, in his **Bāb al-Muwāda'a**, employs and analyzes these material facts as the constitutive elements in the subject matter of mu'āmalāt (mutual relations) and muwāda'a (treaties) from the standpoint of the doctrine of juristic preference by using the concept of tawassu' (extension).[27] Here, Sarakhsī tries to establish the muwāda'a (treaties) and mu'āmalāt (mutual relations) concerning the aḥkām al-dunyā (worldly affairs) as an autonomous discipline, because such matters are broader and wider in nature and, therefore, in order to broaden the scope of Islamic jurisprudence, one deals with them by the doctrine of juristic preference rather than with the doctrine of systematic reasoning. As a matter of fact, the central aspect of the treaties as the constitutive elememt of 'illa and the basis for the doctrine of juristic preference as it emerges in Sarakhsī's **Bāb al-Muwāda'a** is the discussion regarding the aspects of dhimma (protection) and amān (promise of security) etc., in relation to and consideration of the disparity of territories (tabāyun al-dārayn), which takes into account such kinds of material facts. Here follows a brief overview of these aspects which enter into consideration in the matters of muwāda'a (treaties) and mu'āmalāt (mutual relations):

(i) In his **Bāb al-muwāda'a**, Sarakhsī vigorously subjects mu'āmalāt (mutual relations) and muwāda'a to the well-defined doctrine of juristic preference and claims for the first time, though modestly in the name of Shaybānī, that the promise of security (amān), the subject matter of muwāda'a, is ruled by the doctrine of juristic preference.[28] The promise of security is given on the ground of the doctrine of juristic preference, although such is not the case by the doctrine of systematic reasoning.[29] The muwāda'a (treaties) is to be based on the notion of tawassu' (extension).[30] Sarakhsī asserts here that the reason for such an extension is the disparity of territories (tabāyun al-dārayn). It is true that the notion of disparity of territories was first introduced as Schacht observes,[31] by Abū Ḥanīfa and it can be said that Abū Yūsuf in his **Kitāb al-Kharāj** and Shaybānī in his **Kitāb al-Aṣl** used it. But Sarakhsī is the first to establish it by pronouncing clearly and in no uncertain terms that the disparity of territory has the efficacy of going beyond the disparity of religions regarding the matters of amān (protection)[32] and muwāda'a (treaties). Even the rulings with regard to marriage and inheritance are to be dealt with not by the congruity of religion, but on the basis of contract. The inviolability of religion becomes established only for the one who believes in it; not for the one who does not.[33] The laws of Islam are not applicable to other territories;[34] and, equally, they are under no obligation to Muslims, as in the first place they make treaties with Muslims on the condition that the laws of Islam do not apply to them.[35] The dhimma (protection) is designed for the worldly affairs[36] and here the sole concern is the treaty and to abide by what is agreed on by the treaty. It is incumbent on Muslims to abide by the treaty and not to breach the contract when they enter other territories; nor are Muslims allowed without consent to take any property of those whose territory they enter.[37] Again, according to Sarakhsī, all mutual relations (mu'āmalāt) between two territories are conducted according to their own laws and rules and they vary from one territory to another, as the different territories have their own sovereignty and sovereign power and thus are to be ruled according to their laws.[38] With the acceptance of the concept of disparity of territories, their laws are also recognized. If there is a dispute between two parties from those territories in the territory of Islam, their laws are recognized and it is ruled not according to the laws of the territory of Islam, but according to their laws.[39]

(ii) The concept of mutual reciprocity (mujāzā) constitutes an integral aspect of mutual relations between two territories, as the nature of such relations arising due to the treaties (muwāda'a) demand that both territories deal with each other reciprocally and equally. For example, the revenues in general and as a rule are taken according to what is narrated from 'Omar bin Khaṭṭāb that he ordered tithers to collect one fourth of tithe from the Muslim tradesmen, one-half of tithe from the tradesmen who are dhimmīs (inhabitants of the territory of protection) and one (full) tithe from the tradesmen who are mustā'mins (those who enjoy promise of security from Muslims).[40] But, by way of mutual reciprocity (mujāzā) and allowability, it is determined according to what the authorities in other territories take from the Muslim tradesmen when they pass their territories.[41] If they do not take any tithe from Muslim tradesmen passing their territory, it is also not taken from their tradesmen when they pass the territory of Islam.[42] Equally, in matters of testimony regarding the aḥkām al-dunyā (worldly affairs) and mu'āmalāt (mutual relations), whether their testimony is accepted or not, the rule based on the concept of mutual reciprocity (mujāzā) reigns.[43]

(iii) According to Sarakhsī, the local customs and habits ('āda) of the people of different territories play a great role in the determination of the mutual relations and they also should be given due consideration in the matters of muwāda'a and in determining the conditions stipulated in the promise of security (amān). Sarakhsī brings out, for example, the following cases showing their pertinence:

In general, the inhabitants of the territory of protection (dhimmīs) are under obligation to the laws of Islam in what their mutual relations with Muslims ascribe, except what is exempt in the conduct of dhimma (protection), such as the usufruct of wine, pork and forbidden marriage,[44] and the customs and habits not prohibited by their religion.

In the matters of promise of security (amān), the conditions stipulated are determined according to the custom. If the peace agreement is concluded between Muslims and the enemies on an unconditional specification that they would give their one hundred slaves to the Muslims, it is determined according to what the general custom dictates. If they give other persons in their place, it is not acceptable, since the unconditional specification in the agreement applies to what is generally accepted in practice by custom. Obviously, the recognized practice by custom is that the enemies give their slaves, except if other commodity is recognized in practice by custom.[45] Sometimes, it depends also on the custom of the inhabitants of the territory what designation they apply to certain things such as the weapons under which outer garments and firearm vaults are not included. They are generally designated as household goods and not weapons except when they are worn in the war.[46]

Again, if Muslims conclude the promise of security (amān) with the enemies on the condition that "Muslims turn away from them," then such a condition is determined by the fact that Muslims have left the territory of enemies and reached their place of safety which by custom is considered as the territory of Islam. The specific statement "turn away from them" is determined by the custom and by the general statement restricted to the evidences provided by custom.[47]

(iv) Lastly, the concept of necessity (ḍarūra or ḥājāt as Sarakhsī calls it) and the interests of Muslims can also become determining factors in the mutual relations and mutual agreement of Muslims with other territories. For example, if Muslims are in a weaker position or are in fear from enemies, they are forced and justified by the 'illa as used in the doctrine of juristic preference to conclude the peace treaty rather than annihilate themselves.[48]

In short, Sarakhsī expounds on these various material facts throughout his **Bāb al-Muwāda'a** as they consitute the 'illa (effective reasoning) of the doctrine of juristic preference and shows in the course of systematic analysis how they are employed in the matters of treaties which arise due to the broader nature of the mutual relations of Muslims with other territories and nations.

CHAPTER FOUR

Sarakhsī's Systematization of the Doctrine of Juristic Preference

After establishing the justification for the employment of the doctrine of juristic preference from Sarakhsī's **Mabsūṭ**, now we proceed to investigate how Sarakhsī develops and systematizes his doctrine of juristic preference in his **Uṣūl al-Fiqh.** Sarakhsī examines here the various aspects of apparent (ẓāhir) and concealed (bāṭin) 'illa in the forms of wujūh al-iḥtijāj (grounds of what is binding), ta'līl (inference) and tarjīḥ (preference). Sarakhsī's main contention is that the 'illa employed in these forms by the doctrine of juristic preference is connected with the aṣl (Origin), otherwise null and void.

Sarakhsī's main objective is to demonstrate and show the ways in which the 'illa used in these various forms is connected with the aṣl (Origin) and specify the conditions to meet the criteria of its being connected with the aṣl (Origin). Sarakhsī examines and analyzes the various aspects of apparent (ẓāhir) and concealed (bāṭin) 'illa in these forms at great length, mainly because in the controversy regarding the validity of the doctrine of juristic preference, the criticisms by the jurists from other schools of thought center around these aspects of the 'illa of the doctrine.

Therefore, before we proceed to show how Sarakhsī develops and systematizes his doctrine of juristic preference, it would be helpful to mention briefly without any detailed elaboration the main points of criticism which surfaced in the course of the historical development of Islamic jurisprudence against the 'illa employed in these three forms in the doctrine of juristic preference as we shall discuss later in Chapter Six.

1. When the advocates of the doctrine of juristic preference use the wujh (ground), they emphasize one wujh (ground) regarding the 'illa they employ and ignore the other wujūh (grounds).
2. In the ta'līl (inference), the 'illa in one judgment (ḥukm) may not carry the same waṣf (quality or characteristic) or sameness of judgments (jins al-aḥkām) or sameness of things (jinsīya) when used in other judgments (aḥkām).
3. When the tarjīḥ (preference) is given to one qiyās (systematic reasoning) or ḥukm (judgment) over the other, it is ẓann (speculation), shahwā (personal liking) or ra'y (personal discretion) on the part of the one who exercises the istiḥsān (juristic preference).

Keeping this in mind, we now proceed to show how Sarakhsī examines and analyzes the 'illa employed in the forms of (i) wujūh al-iḥtijāj (grounds of what is binding), (ii) ta'līl (inference) and (iii) tarjīḥ (preference) of the doctrine of juristic preference by showing that the 'illa employed in it is strong (qawī) although concealed (khafī or jalīy) as against the 'illa which is appparent (ẓāhir) but weak (ḍa'īf) of the doctrine of systematic reasoning.

(I) The wujūh al-iḥtijāj (Grounds of What is Binding):

The wujh specifically refers to the ground used in the 'illa for the validity of any judgment, whether affirmative or negative. Sarakhsī states that the wujh (ground) does not become binding unless the evidence (dalīl) is provided.[1] Such an evidence (dalīl) of the wujh (ground) should be examined from the point of view of ma'ānī (inward meaning) rather than simple ṣūra (outward form). Sarakhsī goes to the root by inquiring into the nature of the ground (wujh) which forces binding when employed as an 'illa in any judgment and specifies that it should refer to the aṣl (Origin) by evidence. Sometimes, 'illa is claimed to continue to be held as valid especially in the doctrine of systematic reasoning, because there is no evidence shown which nullifies it. Sarakhsī demonstrates this by examining the case of a slave regarding his emancipation (i'tāq). The original owner has the right to purchase the slave from the second owner prior to others and his claim to purchase the slave prior to others is held as valid by the doctrine of systematic reasoning. But, when one examines from the point of view of ma'ānī (inward meaning) on the ground (wujh) of what is binding in the judgment such is not found to be the case, because when the evidence (dalīl) is examined, it proves differently. It is only according to the doctrine of systematic reasoning that the prior right of the original owner to purchase the slave is continued to be held as being valid because, in such (an affirmative) judgment (ḥukm), there is no evidence shown against it. When one inquires and examines on the ground (wujh) of what is binding in light of the evidence (dalīl), especially when it deals with the slave whose emancipation (i'tāq) has the priority, then such is not held as valid. As a matter of fact, the ground (wujh) used as an 'illa in the doctrine of systematic reasoning is nullified on the basis of the evidence by the inward meaning (ma'ānī); as in the testimony that someone purchased the slave and set him free and, thereafter, the original owner appears, then by the doctrine of systematic reasoning, he has the prior right to purchase the slave, but according to the doctrine of juristic preference the slave cannot be given in his guardianship (walāya). Therefore, the 'illa in the (affirmative) judgment used in the doctrine of systematic reasoning which continues to be held as valid now becomes nullified by the doctrine of juristic preference which examines the wujh (ground) of what is binding by evidence. By the evidence (dalīl) seen in the doctrine of juristic preference, the emancipation of the slave carries more weight and is considered much more important on the ground (wujh) of which the 'illa of the doctrine of juristic preference is considered strong (qawī), although concealed (bāṭin), as against the 'illa of the doctrine of systematic reasoning which is apparent (ẓāhir), but weak (ḍa'īf). Here, in the doctrine of juristic preference, the 'illa on the ground (wujh) of what is binding (iḥtijāj) by evidence (dalīl) is seen ḟrom the wider perspective of aḥkām al-dunyā (worldly affairs) in juxtaposition with the doctrine of juristic preference. As explained by Sarakhsī, evidence (dalīl) for the ground (wujh) of what is binding in the judgment for the prior right of ownership to the original owner is not an evidence on accord of which the original owner can keep the ownership, but an evidence which nullifies the keeping of his ownership.[2]

Thus, by analyzing the wujūh al-iḥtijāj (the grounds of what is binding), Sarakhsī is able to demonstrate and show that the doctrine of juristic preference does not emphasize one ground (wujh) at the cost of other grounds (wujūh), as the critics of the doctrine of juristic preference maintain, but rather on the consideration of material facts as the nature of Islamic jurisprudence demands, as the case of emancipation of the slave which enters into account and forces the rejection of the 'illa of the doctrine of systematic reasoning on the ground (wujh) of what is binding by the evidence derived from the aṣl (Origin).

(II) The ta'līl (Inference):

Sarakhsī examines the aspects of apparent (ẓāhir) and concealed (bāṭin) 'illa as used in arriving at an inference, formulating them in terms of 'illa (effective reasoning) and ma'lūl (what is inferred in a judgment as a consequence of an 'illa). Everything remaining the same, the judgment (ḥukm) is to be analyzed by considering the evidence (dalīl), whether as a result of using the apparent (ẓāhir) 'illa or concealed (bāṭin) 'illa. Sarakhsī explains this by giving an example, although from the aḥkām al-dīn (religious affairs) that in prayers what is apparent (ẓāhir) 'illa in a judgment in the first bowing (rukū') is taken as ma'lūl (what is inferred as a consequence of an 'illa) and used as a concealed (bāṭin) 'illa in the second bowing and, if both of them are used as the 'illa, they are considered equivalent provided all other things remain the same in both cases. Another example given by Sarakhsī is from the 'ibāda (religious observance). If fasting (ṣaum) is considered as the 'ibāda, so should be considered the pilgrimage (ḥajj). There is no change in the judgment whatsoever, as both the fasting (ṣaum) and pilgrimage (ḥajj) fall under the same sanctions (aḥkām) as the 'ibādā (religious observance). When one uses the apparent (ẓāhir) 'illa of fasting (ṣaum) in the judgment and what is inferred (ma'lūl) from it is used as a concealed (bāṭin) 'illa in the case of pilgrimage (ḥajj) to arrive at an inference, then there is no change, but rather one infers here by applying what is 'illa in the first case and using what is inferred (ma'lūl) from it as an 'illa in the second case.[3] In both cases, the sameness of sanctions (aḥkām) is evident by examining the apparent (ẓāhir) 'illa in the judgment of one sanction with the judgment in the other sanction where what is inferred (ma'lūl) from the first case as a consequence is used as an 'illa in the second case, though it is concealed (bāṭin). In the first case, the 'illa is apparent (ẓāhir) and, in the second case what is inferred (ma'lūl) from the first case and is used as an 'illa in the second case, is concealed (bāṭin), but in both cases the 'illa is based on the ground (wujh) of what is binding by evidence (dalīl). From this it becomes evident, what Sarakhsī means is, that the ma'ānī (inward meaning) is the sole criteria of any 'illa, whether apparent (ẓāhir) or concealed (bāṭin), in any judgment on the basis of evidence (dalīl) and on the force of which the validity of an inference (ta'līl) is determined.

In his discussion of ta'līl, Sarakhsī also takes into account the aspect of waṣf (characteristic or quality) of an 'illa which is defined here in terms of having sameness of characteristic or quality of an 'illa which is used as an apparent (ẓāhir) 'īlla in a judgment and afterward used as a concealed (bāṭin) 'illa in the subsequent judgments.[4] For example, fasting is accompanied by intention and that is equally applicable when one observes the fasting by qaḍā' (the fasting that makes up for the original fasting which could not have been fulfilled), since both of them carry the same characteristic or quality (i.e. fasting) which is employed in the second case as a concealed (bāṭin) 'illa what was an apparent (ẓāhir) 'illa in the first case. There is nothing extra added to it. Such an addition, if it is provided, is simply what is concealed (bāṭin) 'illa and is the explanation of the judgment (ḥukm) on the ground of the acceptance of evidence (dalīl) and not any changes made therein by ẓann (speculation).[5] It is the strength due to the sameness of the waṣf (characteristic or quality) inferred from a judgment and used in the subsequent judgments. Another example which Sarakhsī cites is the case of performing the ritual of ablution (wuḍū') before the prayer in which one does masḥa (cleaning around the head three times with water) and if one takes a bath, it becomes included in what is required in the ritual of ablution (wuḍū') and thus masḥa is not necessary after taking a bath. This waṣf (characteristic or quality) is used as an 'illa in both of the cases. In the first case, the 'illa is ẓāhir (apparent) and in the second bāṭin (concealed); but, in both cases, it carries the same waṣf (characteristic or quality).[6]

The cases of opposite ('aks) 'illa in judgments deal with when the bāṭin (concealed) 'illa is made as the ẓāhir (apparent) 'illa in a given judgment and this ẓāhir (apparent) 'illa is made as the bāṭin (concealed) 'illa in terms of what is inferred (ma'lūl) and is considered as the 'illa (effective reasoning) and the (original) 'illa is considered as being the ma'lūl (what is inferred). Sarakhsī explains this where in a judgment the opposite of an 'illa results as a negation of it and is seen as ma'lūl (what is inferred from it) by inward meaning (ma'ānī) and since this opposite of 'illa as a mā'lūl becomes established, it is in no way considered as invented by ẓann (speculation) and as if not provided as an 'illa on the basis of evidence (dalīl) in the aṣl (Origin). For example, in the case of supererogatory (nāfila) fasting, if one takes a vow to observe fasting, it becomes obligatory by sharī'a law and the opposite of this 'illa as the ma'lūl results; that is to say, if anyone does not take a vow for fasting, it does not become obligatory, since it is the opposite of what was obligatory and is the result and ma'lūl (what is inferred) of the 'illa used in which the fasting is considered as obligatory.[7]

Sarakhsī discusses the aspect of contraries (mu'āraḍa) in the 'illa employed in arriving at an inference (ta'līl). The contraries in the 'illa are defined here in reference to their being contrary to the 'illa which is based on the aṣl (Origin) by evidence (dalīl) and tries to ascertain in which cases such contraries in the 'illa can be valid and in other cases not valid.

Sarakhsī devides contraries into two groups:
(i) the contraries concerning the 'illa from the aṣl (Origin)
(ii) the contraries concerning judgments of furū' (branches of law).

Sarakhsī discusses them very briefly as follows:

(i) The contraries concerning the 'illa from the aṣl (Origin):

There are three kinds of contraries concerning the 'illa from the aṣl (Origin): first when the contrary described by 'illa from the aṣl (Origin) does not transcend the furū' (branches of law); second when the contrary described by 'illa transcends judgments in the branches of law (furū') and the 'illa in both cases do not differ from one another; and, lastly, when the contraries described by the 'illa transcend judgments in the branches of law and the 'illa in both cases differ from one another.

Sarakhsī does not expound further on these aspects of contraries,[8] since it is obvious that the 'illa based on the aṣl transcends the furū' (branches of law) itself and all its aspects in detail. Sarakhsī's focus is on the examination and analysis of the nature of 'illa and, before it is employed in the sharī'a law, one needs to determine with certainty that the 'illa is based on and connected with the aṣl (Origin) and is not accepted without being properly examined, as in some cases one finds with those who hold fast on the doctrine of systematic reasoning.

(ii) The contraries concerning judgments of furū‘ (branches of law):

There are five kinds of contraries concerning the judgments of furū‘: first the contrary based on the textual evidence against the judgment of an ‘illa in a specific case, as in the case of repeating of masḥa (three times washing around the head by hands) which one has to perform in the ablution (wuḍū’), but is not necessary in the major ritual of ablution (ghusal)[9] and in this case, contrary to what is considered as necessary by the textual evidence in the first case, is valid, since obviously the masḥa (three times washing around the head by hands) becomes already inclusive when one performs the major ritual of ghusal (washing of the whole body).

The second kind of contrary occurs when there is a change which is the explanation of that judgment (ḥukm) on the ground (wujh) of which it was acknowledged. Sarakhsī explains this again with the example of ablution (wuḍū’) wherein the three times washing around the head by hands is considered as necessary in the ablution (wuḍū’), and completion in the required measure is not mandatory in the major ritual of washing the body (ghusal). This contrary is an explanation for the change in the acknowledged judgment (ḥukm).[10]

The two arguments given in the above cases necessitate the contrary for its preference (tarjīḥ) to hold it as being valid, for with the validity of the contrary follows its preference (tarjīḥ).[11]

The third kind of contrary is where there exists a disorder in the posited case. For example, the case of a minor without a father or grandfather in the appointment of a patron and whether he can be given in the guardianship (walāya) of his brother. Here the issue is regarding the guardianship of an orphan to a relative and the ‘illa on which it is based is used as a contrary to the ‘illa in the judgment which negates the guardianship by the specific person (i.e. brother). But, Sarakhsī maintains that in this posited case, the establishment of guardianship by any relative whether father, grandfather, or any other relative like brother is considered the same. This contrary is valid, although Sarakhsī says it is not strong.[12]

The fourth kind of contrary occurs when the sameness or equality (taswīya) of the ‘illa used as contrary is not found connected in the posited inference (ta‘līl).

For example, if an unbeliever purchases a slave who is Muslim, then the slave becomes property of the unbeliever by the conclusion of contract of purchase and upon the slave being taken into possession. Thus, formally a slave can be considered to be the property of the unbeliever when the contract of purchase is concluded and upon the slave being taken into possession. But, according to Sarakhsī, there is a contrary found in this case, that is, the sameness or equality (taswīya) between the original contract of the purchase of a slave and the condition of his being taken into possession do not become connected in the posited inference (ta'līl). Sarakhsī does not expound further on this point, but it is obvious that in the first place the unbeliever is not allowed to purchase a slave who is Muslim, especially in the territory of Islam. Examined from the standpoint of wujh (ground) and on the basis of the jinsīya (sameness of things), this inference (ta'līl) lacks to connect the contrary used as an 'illa in the required manner with the aṣl (Origin) and needs to be taken into account in the posited case.[13]

Lastly, the case of contrary used as an 'illa can be seen in establishing a judgment (ḥukm) which is not suitable. The example is as Abū Yūsuf says, that if a woman intends to divorce her husband and she observes the waiting period ('idda) from him and then marries another person and begets a child from him and, thereafter, the first husband appears, then the lineage of the child in this case is considered as being established from the first husband and not from the second husband. But, Abū Ḥanīfa and Abū Yūsuf maintain that on the basis of 'illa whether the marriage with the second husband is acknowledged as being valid or not has nothing to do with the issue under consideration.

Abū Ḥanifa and Abū Yūsuf do not give any systematic explanation for their views. This could be due to the fact that it was still early in the development of the history of Islamic jurisprudence to analyze the issue under consideration in any systematized form on the doctrinal basis by which they could have provided any explanation in a proper manner. Sarakhsī explains this case by first asserting that any 'illa used in arriving at an inference (ta'līl) in a given judgment (ḥukm) should be connected with the aṣl (Origin) by evidence (dalīl) and here in this case if a woman has observed the waiting period ('idda) from her first (divorced) husband and, thereafter, marries another person and begets a child, now the appearance of the first husband has nothing to do with the lineage of the child. According to the doctrine of systematic reasoning, it is held that the appearance of the first husband still entitles him to the lineage of the child, but when one analyzes this case from the point of view of contrary used as an 'illa, such an inference (ta'līl) fails to connect it with the aṣl (Origin) and, therefore, it is considered by Sarakhsī as ilghā' (null and void). Thus, as seen in this case, the condition of any valid inference (ta'līl) in any judgment (ḥukm) is that the contrary as an 'illa should necessarily be connected with the aṣl (Origin), otherwise it is not valid.[14]

(III) The tarjīḥ (Preference):

The term tarjīḥ (preference) refers obviously to the 'illa (effective reasoning) on the basis of aṣl (Origin) by evidence (dalīl). Sarakhsī first discusses it in relation to the doctrine of qiyās (systematic reasoning) and maintains that when the waṣf (characteristic or quality) employed as an 'illa in a given judgment is found to be directed to what is intended by the aṣl (Origin), then it is given preference and is not considered as something added by ẓann (speculation), as for example in the case of a donation (ṣadaqa). If something is given as a donation (ṣadaqa), it is considered in terms of waṣf (characteristic or quality) used as an 'illa which is intended by the aṣl (Origin), unlike the case of giving ten darhams for one darham out of the goodness of one's heart which can be considered as the waṣf (characteristic or quality), but it has no resemblance to the previous case. If any outward form (ṣūra) of resemblances to the waṣf (characteristic or quality) are added in any judgment (ḥukm), it is not given preference on the ground (wujh) that it is not binding by the aṣl (Origin), as it does not carry the validity of waṣf (characteristic or quality) of the inward meaning (ma'ānī) intended by the aṣl (Origin). For example, in the case of a testimony, if anyone brings two witnesses for his claim in a dispute and his opponent brings four witnesses, then the testimony of the opponent is not preferred simply because it is accompanied by four witnesses, as the judgment (ḥukm) is established by two witnesses and is binding by the aṣl (Origin). However, tarjīḥ is given when one brings two witnesses who are 'udūl (positively known to be of good and veracious character) and the other brings the witnesses who are mastūr (those who have simply blameless records).[15] The testimony accompanied by the witnesses who are 'udūl is given preference over and against the testimony accompanied by the witnesses who are mastūr, because it strengthens the 'illa in its waṣf (characteristic or quality) in a given judgment (ḥukm) on the basis of what is intended by the inward meaning (ma'ānī) and directed to what is considered binding by the aṣl (Origin).

After this general discussion of tarjīḥ (preference) in relation to the doctrine of qiyās (systematic reasoning), Sarakhsī proceeds to relate it to the doctrine of istiḥsān (juristic preference). There are four grounds on which tarjīḥ (preference) can be made in the doctrine of juristic preference (istiḥsān): (i) the strength of evidence (ii) the strength of evidence in a judgment which is acknowledged (iii) when numerous uṣūl (principles) are found and, lastly (iv) preference (tarjīḥ) occurs in the absence of any judgment (ḥukm) with the absence of 'illa.

As to the first case, tarjīḥ (preference) is made on the ground of certainty of waṣf (characterisitic or quality) which is considered as being binding by evidence. Priority is given to the certainty of waṣf (characteristic or quality) which provides the binding of a judgment by strong evidence, like in the case of evidence by the doctrine of juristic preference (istiḥsān) accompanied by the doctrine of systematic reasoning (qiyās); or, when there is a conflict in the narrations, the priority is given to the narration according to whether the narrator mentioned in the chain of narration (riwāya) is reliable and known and not simply how far the chain of narration reaches closer to the Prophet.[16] Here the waṣf (characteristic or quality) of reliability and how the narrator mentioned in the chain of narration is known is considered more certain by evidence, as it strengthens the 'illa and, hence, is preferable. This is based on the strength of evidence which refers back to the uṣūl (principles).[17]

As to the second case, tarjīḥ (preference) is given on the ground of the strength of the acknowledged judgment established on the basis of aṣl (Origin) by the textual evidence (naṣṣ) or ijmā' (general consensus). Thus, whatever becomes established by the textual evidence (naṣṣ) or ijmā' (general consensus) is considered firmly established, and so from that aspect whatever is considered as having more strength in evidence on the basis of uṣūl (principles) becomes preferable, and, on that basis the tarjīḥ (preference) becomes binding. For example, if one gives charity making it as the ṣadaqa (alms) to the poor, it is not considered as the alms tax (zakāt) according to what is established by the naṣṣ (textual evidence) and ijmā' (general consensus). The condition of intention as the waṣf (characteristic or quality) is established by the textual evidence (naṣṣ) and the ijmā' (general consensus) and is given preference to nullify the validity for using what is given in charity as the ṣadaqa (alms) for the alms tax (zakāt) which should be accompanied by the condition of intention as a waṣf (characteristic or quality) for that purpose.[18]

In the third case, the tarjīḥ (preference) is given when it is accompanied by several uṣūl (principles) and in this sense it is considered as the waṣf (characteristic or quality) which is binding as in the case of narration which is well known and hence considered as obligatory to accept it.[19]

The fourth case is when the tarjīḥ (preference) is made in the absence of any judgment (ḥukm) with the absence of 'illa. Sarakhsī considers it the weakest ground of tarjīḥ (preference), because it is possible that the 'illa which is absent could have served as an evidence to establish the connection between the judgment and the 'illa and thus provided the certainty of evidence in the judgment.[20]

Sarakhsī describes general procedure for the above-mentioned cases to avoid any conflicts in establishing the validity of the 'illa on the basis of evidence, for its preference (tarjīḥ) in the following manner:

Every occurrence takes place in a certain outward form (ṣūra) and in reference to its inward meaning (ma'ānī). The circumstances occur and if the evidence of preference contradicts a certain inward meaning (ma'ānī), then the preference is given to the inward meaning (ma'ānī) itself. This is because of two reasons:

(i) The inward meaning (ma'ānī) is more readily available than the circumstances or conditions, so that after preference (tarjīḥ) has taken place, then the inward meaning (ma'ānī) does not change by what has occurred.

(ii) The occurrence takes place with the meaning (ma'ānī) which is based on the aṣl (Origin) and what takes place with it is simply circumstances or conditions which are viewed as subordinate to the aṣl (Origin). The aṣl (Origin) in itself does not change and is not subordinated to any circumstances or conditions.[21]

After this, Sarakhsī concludes that the following kinds of tarjīḥ (preference) are null and void:

The first kind of invalid preference is: (a) One qiyās is given preference to another qiyās, because the 'illa of both is based validly on the aṣl (Origin) by evidence. (b) One of the qiyās when it is given preference to the other on the basis of narration (khabar) is considered as invalid, for if one qiyās is abandoned in favor of the other, it is not binding to prefer one over the other, because the contradiction has already occurred. (c) Likewise, preference of one of the narratives (khabar) in the Text (naṣṣ) is invalid, for it is not binding when contradictions are found in the Text itself.[22]

The second kind of invalid preference is when it is accompanied by several resemblances. The example of such a resemblance is: a brother resembles his father in relation of consanguinity precluding marriage (maḥramīya) and this resemblance is compared with the resemblance to his nephew wherein the requital from both sides, the acceptance of testimony from each for one another and the permissibility of giving alms tax to each other are considered valid.[23] In other words, what is established as invalid in one case because of the resemblance cannot be considered as valid by comparing it with what is established as valid because of the resemblance in the other case.

The third kind of invalid preference is when the 'illa used in the judgment is too general and the inference is concerned with the specific. If priority is given to the general without determining under which category (ṣīghā) the specific falls and the 'illa (effective reasoning) belonging to that particular category (ṣīghā) is not connected properly with the specific under consideration, then such a tarjīḥ (preference) is considered as being invalid, because establishing a judgment by 'illa is a part of connecting the specific to the 'illa based on the naṣṣ (textual evidence) in all the furū' (branches of law) in a required manner.[24] Thereby, the specific becomes determined by the characteristic or quality (waṣf) by falling under the category (ṣīgha) of the sameness of judgments (jins al-aḥkām) and sameness of things (jinsīya).

The last kind of invalid preference is when sufficient auṣūf (pl.of waṣf, characteristics or qualities) are not provided in the judgment. Here, Sarakhsī sums up as a conclusion and as the main contention of the entire discussion by stating that, as a general principle, the 'illa should be accompanied by sufficiency of auṣāf (characteristics or qualities) based on exact and specific textual evidence.[25]

With this, it becomes evident that Sarakhsī systematizes and constructs the doctrine of juristic preference by analyzing its 'illa in the forms of wujūh al-iḥtijāj, ta'līl and tarjīḥ taking into consideration the various aspects of waṣf (characteristic or quality). According to Sarakhsī, for the derivation of any judgment by the doctrine of juristic preference, the 'illa on which it is based should carry the sameness of judgments (jins al-aḥkām) and the sameness of things (jinsīya) cogently with all the specifications required for it to be valid within the framework of sharī'a law and is based on the ground (wujh) of its being binding by evidence (dalīl).

Although Sarakhsīs doctrine of istiḥsān (juristic preference) is analyzed and systematized in both the aḥkām al-dīn (religious affairs) and aḥkām al-dunyā (worldly affairs), it can be noted from the foregoing discussion that in the aḥkām al-dīn (religious affairs), Sarakhsī does not deviate much from the opinions and views held in the traditional Islamic jurisprudence, except only that he examines them afresh from the point of view of the doctrine of juristic preference. From this, one can conclude that Sarakhsī's main concern is to subject the contents of mu'āmalāt, (mutual relations) and muwāda'a (treaties) concerning the aḥkām al-dunyā (worldly affairs) in juxtaposition with the doctrine of juristic preference (istiḥsān) by taking into account all the material facts as the nature of Islamic jurisprudence demands.

CHAPTER FIVE

Sarakhsi's Doctrine of Juristic Preference as a Methodological Approach toward Treaties and Mutual Relations concerning Worldly Affairs and its Consequences

In this Chapter, we shall investigate how Sarakhsī brings out his doctrine of juristic preference (istiḥsān) as developed in his **Uṣūl al-Fiqh** in conjunction and juxtaposition with the subject matter of muwāda'a (treaties) from his **Bāb al-Muwāda'a** and the other material facts or what we have called the constitutive elements from the siyar (Conduct) of his **Mabsūṭ**, which provides the general framework and the contents of muwāda'a (treaties) and mu'āmalāt (mutual relations) of Muslims with other nations concerning the aḥkām al-dunyā (worldly affairs).

We shall first examine and analyze the specific ways in which Sarakhsī relates and brings the subject matter of mu'āmalāt (mutual relations) and muwāda'a (treaties) in juxtaposition with the doctrine of juristic preference; and, second, show how Sarakhsī employs various material facts as the constitutive elements forming a general framework for the contents of muwāda'a (treaties) and mu'āmalāt (mutual relation).

Thus, when the subject matter of muwāda'a (treaties) and mu'āmalāt (mutual relations) concerning the aḥkām al-dunyā (worldly affairs) is brought in juxtaposition with the doctrine of juristic preference, it sheds a different light on Sarakhsī's methodological approach, which is radically different not only in its premise, but also in the conclusions which follow from such a methodological approach. Sarakhsī's methodological approach toward the subject is different from his predecessors, especially Shaybānī to whom his works are generally attributed.

Here we shall discuss the differences not only in their doctrinal approaches, but also in the conclusions which follow from it.

Section I: METHODOLOGIGAL DIFFERENCES BETWEEN SHAYBĀNĪ AND SARAKHSĪ IN THEIR DEVELOPMENT OF SIYAR (CONDUCT)

As already mentioned in Chapter Four, the siyar (Conduct) was developed to broaden the scope of mutual relations (mu'āmalāt) of Muslims with other nations. Initially, it began to develop the regulations for concluding the treaties, their terminations and suspensions and the rules concerning the movements of individuals from one territory to another, the exchange of captives, diplomatic immunity and levying of taxes on the grounds of mutual reciprocity and commensurability. The siyar (Conduct), thus, gradually began to evolve as a separate branch based on the Sunna and local practices, which are equivalent to customs ('āda); the Qur'ān, the utterances of the Prophet and Caliph's decisions and instructions which represent authority (āthār); the principles and rules enshrined in treaties with other nations which fall under the category of agreements ('ahad and muwāda'a); and, finally, the juristic writings which are considered as based on the analogical deduction (qiyās) and other forms of reasoning, such as ra'y (personal discretion) and istiḥsān (juristic preference), in accordance with the Islamic legal methodology .[1]

In the beginning, as we find in Shaybānī's works, the siyar (Conduct) was derived largely from customs and to a certain extent from reasoning based on the legal juristic methodology of qiyās (systematic reasoning), but we do not find much use of istiḥsān (juristic preference). In the siyar (Conduct) of **Kitāb al-Aṣl**, Shaybānī combines analogy (qiyās) and traditions (aḥādīth) and presents large collections of traditions.[2] He is content to present the siyar material as it was conceived and understood in the Ḥanafī school of thought at that time. There is no extensive use of reasoning based on legal methodology in Shaybānī's siyar (Conduct) of **Kitāb al-Aṣl**. Shaybānī does not make a clear distinction between the qiyās (systematic reasoning) and istiḥsān (juristic preference), much less conceive them as two doctrines different in their nature, purpose and methodological approach. This might be attributed to the fact that it was a formative period for the development of siyar (Conduct) and it was not yet developed in its complete form as one finds it later during the time of Sarakhsī.

The clear definition of the siyar (Conduct) is given first by Sarakhsī stating its concise subject matter, conceiving of it as an extension of the sharī'a law wherein Sarakhsī employs the doctrine of istiḥsān (juristic preference) by using the concept of tawassu' (extension) to include in the siyar (Conduct) the subject matter of muwāda'a (treaties) and mu'āmal'āt (mutual relations) of Muslims with other nations in the aḥkām al-dunyā (worldly affairs). As far as such a methodological approach based on legal methodology is concerned, we do not find in Shaybānī's works any distinction between the doctrine of qiyās (systematic reasoning) and the doctrine of istiḥsān (juristic preference), whereas Sarakhsī, keeping in mind the nature and purpose of siyār (Conduct) finds the doctrine of istiḥsān (juristic preference) a very viable and the most essential methodological approach. Sarakhsī establishes its 'illa (effective reasoning) based on and connected with the aṣl (Origin) for the justification of the doctrine of juristic preference (istiḥsān) independently of the doctrine of systematic reasoning (qiyās).

When we examine Shaybānī's siyar (Conduct) from his **Kitāb al-Aṣl** with the accounts of Sarakhsī's siyar of the **Mabsūṭ** and **Bāb al-Muwāda'a** concerning the subject matter of muwāda'a (treaties) and mu'āmalāt (mutual relations) in conjunction and juxtaposition with the doctrine of juristic preference (istiḥsān), we find striking differences inspite of the fact that both deal with the same subject matter. Shaybānī's account of siyar (Conduct) in his **Kitāb al-Aṣl** is, generally speaking, in terms of the prevalent view of the second century Hijra calendar (eighth century A.D.). He mostly presents the traditions (aḥādīth) in the contents of his account of siyar (Conduct) and in his **Jami' al-Ṣaghīr**, there is only one small section devoted to the siyar (Conduct) in which he discusses the case of apostates and their joining the enemy territory.[3] As already mentioned, Shaybānī's **Kitāb al-Siyar al-Kabīr** whose original text seems to have been lost, is known to us through the elaborate commentary of Sarakhsī's **Sharḥ al-Siyar al-Kabīr**, which virtually amounts to a new book and represents the Ḥanafī doctrines as they were understood in the fifth century of the Islamic era (eleventh century A.D.).[4] Although it may be regarded as an exposition of Shaybānī's siyar (Conduct) as Sarakhsī understood him (Shaybānī), in fact it is Sarakhsī's own presentation of siyar (Conduct) vigorously subjected to and interpreted in juxtaposition with the doctrine of juristic preference (istiḥsān). Thus, in the **Bāb al-Muwāda'a**, it is not Shaybānī's views that Sarakhsī is representing as attributed by Kruse,[5] but rather it is Sarakhsī's own account of siyar interpreted in juxtaposition with the doctrine of juristic preference as developed by Sarakhsīin his **Uṣūl al-Fiqh** and **Mabsūṭ**. Thus, it is the doctrinal approach which sets Sarakhsī apart from Shaybānī. It is true that Shaybānī to a certain extent uses the istiḥsān (what is preferable), but in Shaybānī's accounts of siyar (Conduct), there is no conscious effort found to establish the 'illa (effective reasoning) employed in the form of istiḥsān as the juristic reasoning connected with the aṣl (Origin), whereas Sarakhsī's accounts of siyar (Conduct) in his **Mabsūṭ** and **Bāb al-Muwāda'a** are presented according to the doctrine of juristic preference by justifying the 'illa (effective reasoning) employed on the basis of aṣl (Origin). This can be shown by analyzing the following two cases where Shaybānī uses the term istiḥsān (what is preferable) and comparing them with how Sarakhsī explains that the 'illa (effective reasoning) in the various forms of the doctrine of juristic preference (istiḥsān) is being connected in a specific way with the aṣl (Origin).

In Shaybānī's entire text of the siyar (Conduct) of the **Kitāb al-Aṣl**, we find that the term istiḥsān (and for that matter even the term qiyās) is used in two cases. In the first case, Shaybānī even does not make any distinction between the terms qiyās and istiḥsān. In the second case, he does not try to justify the use of the doctrine of juristic preference on the ground that its 'illa (effective reasoning) is connected with the aṣl (Origin). It is at most ra'y (personal discretion), if not quite arbitrary.

The first case deals with the situation in which a male or female captive fell in a collective lot and the warrior set him or her free as his individual share before the division of booty and he or she is considered free; and the other case deals with the situation wherein a slave is set free before the division of booty and he is not considered as being free.

According to Shaybānī, these two cases are considered analogically (namely, by the qiyās) as the same, but in the first it is preferable to abandon the analogy (qiyās) and follow istiḥsān (what is preferable) and, thus, the emancipation would be permissible.[6] Thus, the term is here understood as ra'y (personal discretion). It is not used in a technical sense as a doctrine, since Shaybānī does not try to show explicitly how its 'illa (effective reasoning) is connected with the aṣl (Origin). In contrast, if we compare the similar case, as analyzed by Sarakhsī in his **Uṣūl al-Fiqh**, we find that he tries to establish the 'illa (effective reasoning) of the doctrine with the aṣl (Origin) by examining the evidence found in the testimony on the basis of which the slave is considered free: a person testifies that he purchased the slave and set him free and, thereafter, the original owner comes and desires to purchase the slave. Although according to the doctrine of systematic reasoning the original owner has the prior right to purchase the slave before the second owner can sell the slave to anyone, the slave is considered as being free and cannot be given in the guardianship (walāya) of the original owner.[7] If one examines on the basis of evidence provided by the testimony that the slave was set free when dealing with the mu'āmalāt (mutual relations) concerning the aḥkām al-dunyā (worldly affairs), the consideration of the emancipation of a slave carries more importance. Hence, the 'illa (effective reasoning) of the doctrine of systematic reasoning (qiyās) is abandoned in favor of the 'illa (effective reasoning) of the doctrine of juristic preference on the ground of what is binding (wujh al-iḥtijāj) by evidence as provided in the testimony in the case under consideration. Here, Sarakhsī establishes the 'illa (effective reasoning) on the ground of what is binding (wujh al-iḥtijāj) by the doctrine of juristic preference.

The second case under consideration is from Shaybānī's siyar of **Kitāb al-Aṣl** and Sarakhsī's **Bāb al-Muwāda'a**. If a mustā'min (person who enjoys the promise of security from Muslims) dies in the territory of Islam and his heirs come to the territory of Islam with the amān (promise of security or safe conduct), and if they provide the evidence to their claim to the inheritance by the testimony of the inhabitants of dār al-dhimma (territory of protection), then the issue under consideration is if such a testimony is acceptable or not. According to Shaybānī, such a testimony is not accepted on the basis of the doctrine of systematic reasoning, but it is accepted on the basis of istiḥsān (what is preferable).[8] According to Sarakhsī also, it is accepted on the basis of the doctrine of juristic preference (istiḥsān), but he adduces the 'illa (effective reasoning) for its justification by explaining it on the well-defined concept of 'āda (custom), which he uses as a constitutive element of muwāda'a (treaties). Sarakhsī explains that as a custom only the inhabitants of dār al-dhimma (territory of protection) would be able to provide such a testimony, because Muslims living in the territory of Islam would not know the relatives of the deceased. Thus, here, custom in the muwāda'a (treaties) as a constitutive element is employed as an 'illa (effective reasoning) of the doctrine of juristic preference; and, thereby, the 'illa of the doctrine is seen as being justified.[9]

Again, when Sarakhsī deals in his **Mabsūṭ** with the siyar material such as amān (promise of security) in the case of a slave who is Muslim, the issue is whether he is given simple amān (promise of security) or dhimma (protection). According to Sarakhsī, since the slave is Muslim, he must be given dhimma (protection) rather than simple amān (promise of security) and adduces its ʻilla (effective reasoning) on the basis of ḥadīth (tradition) which says: "strive to protect those who are low," and the slaves and women etc., are considered low, they must be given dhimma (protection). Here, the slave's Islam, namely, his being a Muslim, is used as an ʻilla on the basis of the ḥadīth (tradition) and is connected with the aṣl (Origin) and, hence, the justification for his being given dhimma (protection) rather than simple amān (protection) as the dhimma (protection) is better than the amān (promise of security) and he is given the better of the two.[10]

These illustrations suffice to show that although Sarakhsī seems to deal with the siyar material after Shaybānī, in fact, he is subjecting it vigorously in conjunction and juxtaposition with the doctrine of juristic preference and establishes its ʻilla (effective reasoning) on the basis of aṣl (Origin).

Section II: SARAKHSĪ'S INCORPORATION OF MUWĀDAʻA (TREATIES) AND MUʻĀMALĀT (MUTUAL RELATIONS) CONCERNING THE AḤKĀM AL-DUNYĀ (WORLDLY AFFAIRS) IN CONTRAST TO SHAYBĀNĪ'S TREATMENT OF SIYAR (CONDUCT)

Shaybānī's Bāb al-Siyar of his **Kitāb al-Aṣl** deals with siyar material without any focus on the conceptual framework with any defined subject matter. It simply begins with the discussion, "Relations of Muslims with Dār al-Ḥarb (Territory of War) and Dār al-Dhimma (Territory of Protection)" by describing individual instances supported by the aḥādīth (traditions),[11] whereas Sarakhsī in his discussion of siyar (Conduct) in the **Mabsūṭ**, first specifies concisely by stating that the subject matter of siyar material is the muʻāmalāt (mutual relations) of Muslims with other nations and finds its scope within the sharīʻa law and, thus, sets its framework. Such an acute awareness of the issue is simply absent in Shaybānī's works because Shaybānī does not treat the siyar material on any definite doctrinal basis as does Sarakhsī with his doctrine of juristic preference.

This becomes more evident when one looks at Shaybānī's chapter on "Treaties" which is the central aspect of siyar (Conduct). Shaybānī simply deals with the subject matter without taking into consideration the formal and legal framework of the treaties and their nature,[12] whereas Sarakhsī in his **Bāb al-Muwāda'a,** immediately after discussing in the first chapter under what conditions Muslims can conclude peace treaties, deals with the formal structure of muwāda'a (treaties) in the second chapter under the heading "Shurūṭ" (Stipulations) and uses the stipulations as a legal instrument to incorporate the subject matter of muwāda'a (treaties) into the formal structure of sharī'a law by employing the general rules laid down for concluding any legal contracts as specified in the Qur'ān and the Sunna. We shall here explicate the import of Sarakhsī's doctrine of juristic preference in juxtaposition with the subject matter of muwāda'a (treaties) and mu'āmalāt (mutual relations), though at the cost of some repetition of what has already been discussed in Chapters Three and Four.

Sarakhsī first describes the formal condition which the peace agreements should meet in accordance with what is laid down in the Qur'ān and Sunna. In the siyar of **Mabsūṭ**, Sarakhsī states that no stipulations should be made which are against the book of God.[13] In his **Bāb al-Muwāda'a**, Sarakhsī states that if the fulfillment of the agreement is not possible according to the sharī'a law, it is not valid. If the Muslims have concluded such a treaty, it is null and void and thus to be violated. Any conditions in the treaty should not be against the sharī'a law.[14] Here, Sarakhsī also states, as the Qur'ān prescribes, that the treaty concluded between two parties should be reduced to writing, so that the parties concerned know exactly what are the stipulations in the treaty[15] and there remains no room for any ambiguity, misunderstanding or dispute. The contract should be written down in two copies, as the Prophet Muḥammad used to do,[16] so that each party can keep one copy of the treaty and thereby no one can alter it, as each party shall have the evidence to show what is stipulated in the treaty. The treaty should be written in the best possible manner and describe its stipulations with clarity.[17] It should describe all the specifications, such as the time-period for which the treaty is concluded, which day and date does it begin and end.[18] It should also specify the objects, their quantities and qualities made as the stipulations in the treaty.[19] With this it becomes evident that Sarakhsī, unlike Shaybānī, tries to establish the formal structure of muwāda'a (treaties) and its contents directly from the Qur'ān and Sunna for its employment in juxtaposition with the doctrine of juristic preference independently of the doctrine of systematic reasoning.

After incorporating the muwāda'a (treaties) into a formal and legal structure of sharī'a law, now we proceed to show from the chapter of "Shurūṭ (Stipulations) of his **Bāb al-Muwāda'a,** how Sarakhsī sets the 'illa employed in the three forms, wujh (ground), ta'līl (inference) and tarjīḥ (preference) of the doctrine of juristic preference in juxataposition and in congruity with the nature of the subject matter of muwāda'a (treaties) and mu'āmalāt (mutual relations) concerning the aḥkām al-dunyā (worldly affairs) and demonstrate that the consequences which follow from it are different than from the usual approach of the doctrine of systematic reasoning.

The first case to be considered is from the point of view of wujh al-iḥtijāj (ground of what is binding) of the doctrine of juristic preference. If an inhabitant of the territory of war (ḥarbī) asks for the promise of security (amān) on the condition that he would lead the Muslims to the specified number of captives, and he leads Muslims to less than the specified number of captives, then according to the doctrine of systematic reasoning, he is executed as specified by the condition of contract, but not according to the doctrine of juristic preference. Here the consideration is the condition of the contract between the two parties, and the inhabitant of the territory of war has already abided with some parts of the conditions as if he would fulfill the rest of them. Thus, if we weigh this ground (wujh) of the condition, it is not valid to execute him.[20]

The second case to be considered is regarding the designation of the grandchildren and if they are covered under amān (promise of security). According to the doctrine of systematic reasoning only the offspring from a son's lineage are considered as his progeny. But, according to Sarakhsī, this inference (ta'līl) is based on the analogy (qiyās) of inheritance which properly speaking falls under the aḥkām al-dīn (religious affairs), but when one deals with the matters of amān (promise of security) and dhimma (protection), such matters fall under the scope of mu'āmalāt (mutual relations) of Muslims with other nations concerning the aḥkām al-dunyā (worldly affairs) and, hence, based on the 'illa (effective reasoning) in the form of ta'līl (inference) of the doctrine of juristic preference, the grandchildren are covered under the amān (promise of security), since the amān (promise of security) and dhimma (protection) are designed for facilitation and laxity. Based on this material fact which enters into consideration, the 'illa in the form of ta'līl (inference) of the doctrine of juristic preference becomes connected with and justified by the aṣl (Origin).[21]

The third case to be analyzed is that of booty. According to the doctrine of systematic reasoning, the testimony of those persons who have a share in the booty is not accepted, because of their self-interest in it. According to the doctrine of juristic preference, one has to view this from a different and wider perspective and accept their testimony, because the booty is public property which does not prevent us from accepting such a testimony[22] and is given preference by the doctrine of juristic preference abandoning the judgment held by the doctrine of systematic reasoning.

The fourth case is that of designation which can be viewed on the basis of siyar material regarding the amān (promise of security) and dhimma (protection) which are broader and more facilitating in their nature. The case under consideration deals with as to who can be considered as included under the designation of a family member. A family member is generally considered to be the one for whom the head of the house is responsible or it can also mean lineage. In such matters when it deals with the amān (promise of security) or dhimma (protection), designation of a family member is determined which includes both sides according to the doctrine of juristic preference, for the promise of security (amān) or protection (dhimma) are designed for the aḥkām al-dunyā (worldly affairs) and the 'illa (effective reasoning) employed by the doctrine of juristic preference is based on the concept of tawassu' (extension) which takes into account the material facts, such as facilitation and laxity in the aḥkām al-dunyā (worldly affairs). On the other hand, if it had been simply the case of inheritance which, properly speaking, falls under the aḥkām al-dīn (religious affairs), it is to be ruled by the doctrine of systematic reasoning,[23] but according to Sarakhsī, the subject matter of siyar (Conduct) such as "dhimma (protection) is by its very nature based on the notion of tawassu' (extension)."[24]

Thus, as seen here Sarakhsī first shows that all stipulations (shurūṭ) of the muwāda'a (treaties) are made and viewed taking into account the material facts which enter into consideration when one deals with the mu'āmalāt (mutual relations) of Muslims with other nations concerning the aḥkām al-dunyā (worldly affairs) in juxtaposition with the doctrine of juristic preference; and, therefore,

Sarakhsī claims that the matters such as amān (promise of security), 'ahad (peace agreement) and dhimma (protection) are determined and ruled by the doctrine of juristic preference, although such is not the case by the doctrine of systematic reasoning.[25]

Now, we proceed to show, by referring to what has been discussed in Chapter Three, how Sarakhsī encompasses all the material facts what we have called the constitutive elements of muwāda'a (treaties) to broaden the mu'āmalāt (mutual relations) concerning the aḥkām al-dunyā (worldly affairs) making it more facilitating by the doctrine of juristic preference and show how they can be interwoven and embedded in the formal structure of sharī'a law. We shall bring out the import of these constitutive elements of muwāda'a (treaties), which form the general and structural framework and determine the nature and contents of mu'āmalāt (mutual relations) concerning the aḥkām al-dunyā (worldly affairs) in juxtaposition with the doctrine of juristic preference and compare it with Shaybānī's siyar (Conduct) wherever necessary.

The first and foremost integral constitutive element of muwāda'a (treaties) is the concept of tabāyun al-dārayn (disparity of territories). Shaybānī simply begins his siyar in the **Kitāb al-Aṣl** by describing the conduct of Muslims with Dār al-Ḥarb (Territory of War) and Dār al-Dhimma (Territory of Protection) at most by describing the rules and regulations[26] without having any formal and structural focus of the doctrinal approach on the basis of which one can systematize it by a specific concept such as Sarakhsī's concept of tabāyun al-dārayn (disparity of territories) under which all rules and regulations fall and are determined and analyzed by virtue of the 'illa (effective reasoning) and justified by connecting it with the aṣl (Origin). Sarakhsī, in contrast, sets the whole subject matter of the siyar (Conduct) as mu'āmalāt (mutual relations) concerning the aḥkām al-dunyā (worldly affairs) by introducing the specific concept of tabāyun al-dārayn (disparity of territories). Thereby, Sarakhsī makes a clear demarcation between the aḥkām al-dīn (religious affairs) and aḥkām al-dunyā (worldly affairs) and states, "the tabāyun al-dārayn (disparity of territories) has the efficacy of going beyond the disparity of religions with regard to the amān (promise of security)"[27] and such other matters. The laws of Islam are not applicable to other territories[28] when they deal with the mu'āmalāt (mutual relations) of Muslims with other nations concerning the aḥkām al-dunyā (worldly affairs); and equally they are under no obligation to the laws of Islam, as in the first place, they make a peace treaty with the territory of Islam on the condition that the laws of Islam do not apply to them.[29] The dhimma (protection) is designed for the worldly affairs (aḥkām al-dunyā).[30] It is incumbent on Muslims to abide by the (peace) treaty and not breach any contract when they enter other territories; nor are they allowed without consent to take the property of those whose territory they enter.[31] Even the envoys of other territories are under absolute and unconditional protection when they enter the territory of Islam.[32]

With the acceptance of tabāyun al-dārayn (disparity of territories), the political authority of other territories and their laws are also recognized. According to Sarakhsī, all the mu'āmalāt (mutual relations) among them are regulated according to their own laws and rules and they vary from one territory to another, as different territories have their own sovereignty and sovereign power and thus are to be ruled according to their laws.[33]

In short, Sarakhsī views these material facts afresh on a doctrinal basis encompassing and unifying them systematically under the specific concept of tabāyun al-dārayn (disparity of territories) by employing them in juxtaposition with the doctrine of juristic preference rather than describing the rules and regulations simply as isolated instances as Shaybānī does.

The concept of mujāzā (mutual reciprocity) as a specific concept is not found in Shaybānī. He discusses, for example, the case of The Tithe Duties Imposed on the Inhabitants of the Territory of War[34] again as an isolated instance and not regulated by a laid down principle under the specific concept of mujāzā (mutual reciprocity) which can be used as a constitutive element of muwāda'a (treaties) taking into consideration the material facts necessary in the maintenance of mu'āmalāt (mutual relations) of Muslims with other nations as found with Sarakhsī. Sarakhsī bases the mu'āmalāt (mutual relations) on the specific concept of mujāzā (mutual reciprocity)[35] as a constitutive element in the muwāda'a under which rules and regulations are determined by and derived on the basis of the aṣl (Origin) as already explained in Chapter Three.

The local customs and practices ('āda) are recognized when they relate to the stipulations in the peace treaties.[36] For example, the designation of certain commodities such as the household goods is made as the condition in the peace treaty, then by custom its designation is recognized as a condition made textually.[37] Sarakhsī uses 'āda (customs) as a constitutive element of the muwāda'a, whereas in Shaybānī such a consideration of material fact as a constitutive element entering into consideration regarding the mu'āmalāt (mutual relations) is virtually non-existent.

The necessity (ḥāja or ḍarūra) is also an integral part of the peace agreements and muwāda'a (treaties). For example, if Muslims find themselves in a weaker position, they are allowed to conclude a peace agreement with other territories; or if it is in the interest of Muslims, they can conclude a peace treaty with the territory of war (dār al-ḥarb) without asking anything in return for it.[38] But on the other hand, Sarakhsī also takes into account other material facts under ḥāja (necessity) as a formal constitutive element of muwāda'a (treaties), such as the case of meager conditions of the inhabitants of dār al-dhimma (territory of protection), then they are levied jizya (poll tax) according to their capacity; or if the inhabitants of dār al-dhimma (territory of protection) are in need of help from Muslims against enemy attack, Muslims are obliged to help them, as the protection of the inhabitants of dār al-dhimma (territory of protection) is part of the formal treaty.[39]

Finally, in the matters of muwāda'a (treaties) consideration is also given to taufīq (arbitration). For example, if a Muslim of veracious and good character testifies that a seized person is an inhabitant of dār al-ḥarb (territory of war) and the seized person claims that he is a Muslim and not what the witness attests, then he is considered to be a free person according to the doctrine of juristic preference as a result of an arbitration (taufīq) between these two testimonies because it is possible that the inhabitant of dār al-dhimma (territory of protection) might have become Muslim at a later time and the witness does not have knowledge of it.[40] Here the considerations in the doctrine of systematic reasoning and the doctrine of juristic preference are different. In the doctrine of systematic reasoning, as Sarakhsī explains, his Islam, namely, his becoming a Muslim is considered after he was given dhimma (protection), which is simply a contract, but Islam is higher than dhimma (protection). And, when one considers the matter from the point of view of the doctrine of juristic preference, it is possible that the inhabitant of dār al-dhimma (territory of protection) after the contract of dhimma (protection) could have become Muslim.[41] Here laxity, which is embedded in the nature of mu'āmalāt (mutual relations), is taken into account. Hence, when one views the subject matter of mu'āmalāt (mutual relations) in juxtaposition with the doctrine of juristic preference, the consequences which follow from it are different than what is generally held by the doctrine of systematic reasoning. This is simply due to the fact that in the doctrine of systematic reasoning this material fact was not taken into account which the doctrine of juristic preference does.

Thus, encompassing all these material facts as the constitutive elements of muwāda'a in the matters of mu'āmalāt (mutual relations) concerning the aḥkām al-dunyā (worldly affairs), Sarakhsī deals with the subject matter of siyar (Conduct) as an autonomous discipline in juxtaposition with the doctrine of juristic preference to widen and enrich the scope of Islamic jurisprudence within the framework of sharī'a law.

CHAPTER SIX

Sarakhsī's Doctrine of Juristic Preference in the Historical Development of Islamic Jurisprudence and its Significance as a Methodological Approach toward Treaties and Mutual Relations concerning Worldly Affairs

Section I: SARAKHSĪ'S DOCTRINE OF JURISTIC PREFERENCE IN THE CONTEXT OF THE DEVELOPMENT OF ISLAMIC JURISPRUDENCE AND THE CONTROVERSY REGARDING THE DOCTRINE OF JURISTIC PREFERENCE

As already mentioned in the Introduction, the nub of the matter in the historical development of Islamic jurisprudence is the use of ra'y (exercise of reasoning); and, as a consequence, the ra'y (exercise of reasoning) as a methodological approach has been instrumental in the development of Islamic jurisprudence, but at the same time it also has become the matter of controversy. In the earlier stages of the development of Islamic jurisprudence, the Muslim jurists, in most cases, had to fall back on the ra'y (exercise of reasoning) employed in the form of the doctrine of qiyās (systematic reasoning) and also other forms of methodological reasoning such as the istiḥsān (what is preferable) in the Ḥanafī school of thought, the istiṣlāḥ (consideration of what is beneficial or expedient) in the Mālikī school of thought and the istiṣḥāb (the presumption of continuity of judicial or legal situation as it had existed previously, so long as there does not exist any evidence for its discontinuity) in the Ḥambalī school of thought. We find in the juristic deductions from simple origins (viz., the Qur'ān and Ḥadīth or Sunna), that the ra'y (exercise of reasoning) was used and given systematic validity, and thus became a kind of popular element adopted among the constitutive sources agreed on by the ijmā' (general consensus).[1]

With Mālik bin Anas (179 A.H./795 A.D.), who is regarded as the founder of the Ḥijāzī school of thought, we find in the **Muwāṭṭa'** a corpus jurist which is a synthesis of the four roots (namely, the Qur'ān, Sunna, ijmā' and qiyās) of Islamic jurisprudence. Mālik represents in time, a stage in the development of Islamic jurisprudence in which the juristic reasoning is yet not thorough and fundamental and is permeated by a religious and moral point of view. Mālik in his jurisprudence gives preference to the 'amal or Sunna (the actual undoubted practice in Medina) and to the traditions (aḥādīth), but when these practices or traditions did not exist, he laid down the law independently. In other words, he exercised the ra'y (reasoning) and recognized its validity without any restriction and made use of it in establishing legal and juristic preference. In the Mālikī school of thought, such a use of ra'y is considered legitimate and is called the istiṣlāḥ (consideration of what is beneficial or expedient, maṣlaḥa or murā'āt al-aṣlaḥ).[2] On the other hand, in the school of Abū Ḥanīfa (150 A.H./767 A.D.) who is regarded as the founder of the Irāqī school of thought, it was put on a firmer footing by Abū Yūsuf (182 A.H./804 A.H.) and Shaybānī (189 A.H./804 A.D.). The use of ra'y was given a free reign and it was used extensively. A certain amount of freedom was given for the deviation from the usual methodology of qiyās by allowing practical considerations and was called the istiḥsān. The legal authority was justified in deviating from a ruling suggested by the qiyās, if due considerations showed him that another procedure was suitable to the conditions in question.[3] The Ḥanafī school of thought claims that the use of istiḥsān is based on purely material evidences āthār (evidences) provided for in the sharī'a sources and is not the outcome of sheer speculation (ẓann) or personal inclinations (shahwā or mail). But, the Mālikī school of thought claims that it employs the principle based on positive foundation by using the material principle of maṣlaḥa (consideration of what is beneficial or expedient) rather than the formal "founding good" of the doctrine of istiḥsān. In this sense, the istiṣlāḥ is considered by the Mālikī jurists to be more limited and more closely defined by restricting the use of methodological reasoning to the material principle of maṣlaḥa (what is beneficial or expedient).[4]

Thereafter, Shāfi'ī (204 A.H./820 A.D.) systematized the method of reasoning and made its use without prerogatives of the Qur'ān, Sunna, ijmā and qiyās. In the Shafi'ī school of thought, the use of ra'y is limited by strict rules[5] and Ibn Ḥambal (241 A.H./820 A.D) makes concession only under absolute necessity (ḍarūra) and derives where possible, every law from the traditional sources. Thus, in the Ḥambalī school of thought, attempts were made to set aside use of any kind of reasoning (ra'y), since it was considered speculative (ẓannī). This tendency was even more pronounced in the Ẓāhirīya school of thought.[6] Therefore, we shall treat in this Chapter both of these schools and the criticisms of the individual jurists from these schools against the use of ra'y under one group, since the conclusions which follow from their positions are not much different. Nonetheless, it can be said in general that after Ibn Ḥambal both of these schools allowed the use of istiṣḥāb (the presumption of continuity of a judicial or legal situation as it had existed previously, so long as there does not exist any evidence for its discontinuity). As the principle of istiṣḥāb is not the source of positive law which takes into consideration the material facts and to the extent that it is not a means of preserving the rights that have already been established, it does not become the matter of dispute.[7]

Thus, reduced to its naked form, the controversy centers around the validity of ra'y in the form of the doctrine of istiḥsān and the doctrine of istiṣlāḥ. The common threads of defense and criticism in the controversy relate to the validity of the 'illa (effective reasoning) these doctrines employ. The jurists from the Ḥanafī school of thought sought to establish the validity of the doctrine of istiḥsān by construing its 'illa as being strong but connected with the aṣl (Origin) for the purpose of extending the 'illa to what is more accommodating, facilitating and convenient, and thereby, they made every effort to defend against the objections raised by the jurists especially from the Shāfi'ī and Ḥambalī schools of thought. On the other hand, the jurists from the Mālikī school of thought tried to establish the legal methodological reasoning only by the qiyās to the exclusion of ra'y especially in the form of istiḥsān and sought to construe the justification of the doctrine of istiṣlāḥ on the basis of maṣlaḥa (what is beneficial or expedient) by defending against the criticisms raised from the quarters of the Shāfi'ī and Ḥambalī schools of thought. But, too much emphasis should not be placed on this general opinion resulting from the position they held formally. The circles of those who recognize the principle of istiṣlāḥ in practice extends far beyond the Mālikī school of thought.[8] For example, Ghazālī (505 A.H./1111 A.D.) formally belongs to the Shāfi'ī school of thought, but allows the istiṣlāḥ to ease the requirements of the Qur'ān and Sunna in case of necessity (ḍarūra); Ṭūfī (716 A.H./1316 A.D.), and in modern times Riḍā (1246 A.H./1865 A.D.), both of whom belong to the Ḥambalī school of thought, not only recognize maṣlaḥa, but in fact they use it as a main vehicle of legal and juristic reasoning. Ibn

Taymīya (728 A.D./1328 A.H.), who is also formally a Ḥambalī jurist, favors the doctrine of istiḥsān. In the controversy concerning the use of ra'y either in the form of istiḥsān or istiṣlāḥ, the main issue is concerning the validity of the 'illa (effective reasoning) used in the legal methodological reasoning rather than simply the question of to which formal school of thought an individual jurist belongs.

Moreover, after Ghazālī other Shāfi'ī jurists dealt with the issue of istiṣlāḥ, for example, Isnawī (772 A.H./1370 A.D.), Subkī (771 A.H./1370 A.D.), Maḥāllī (864 A.H./1460 A.D.), Bannānī (1198 A.H./1784 A.D.), but they contributed very little that was new. They merely tried to systematize the use of istiṣlāḥ as a methodological reasoning wherein the istiṣlāḥ, like the istiḥsān is increasingly conceived of as a kind of qiyās khafī (concealed or hidden qiyās),[9] in contrast to the more obvious method of deducing legal reasoning based on the qiyās as we find is the case with Subkī. This tendency toward systematization, however, reaches its height in the later works on the **Uṣūl** by Taftāzānī (792 A.H./1390 A.D.), Amīr al-Ḥājj (879 A.H./1474 A.D.),[10] and Sarakhsī, who not only systematizes istiḥsān as a doctrine thoroughly, but also analyzes it to its fullest in juxtaposition with the subject matter of muwāda'a (treaties) and mu'āmalāt (mutual relations) concerning the aḥkām al-dunyā (worldly affairs).

Hence, in the following section, we shall present in chronological order what is seen as appropriate views from the various respresentative jurists from the four schools of thought in order to provide thematic unity to the subject matter and show in general how these criticisms against the doctrine of istiḥsān do not refute Sarakhsī's position.

Section II: CONTROVERSY IN THE HISTORICAL DEVELOPMENT OF THE DOCTRINE OF JURISTIC PREFERENCE AS A METHODOLOGICAL APPROACH IN RELATION TO SARAKHSĪ'S POSITION:

Before we deal with the view on the methodological reasoning in the form of the doctrine of istiḥsān or the doctrine of istiṣlāḥ, it needs to be clarified that the reason for the controversy and misgivings regarding the employment of the doctrine of isthsān in the historical development of Islamic jurisprudence is mostly due to the fact that it was left undefined by its propounders,[11] as we have seen in the cases of Abū Ḥanīfa, Abū Yūsuf and Shaybānī. They used the concept of the doctrine very vaguely, if they did not apply it quite arbitrarily. But, Sarakhsī proceeds with a well-defined concept of the doctrine of juristic preference in his **Mabsūṭ** and analyzes the 'illa of the doctrine of juristic preference in his **Uṣūl** in terms of its being strong (qawī) although concealed (bāṭin) and shows its validity by examining it in the forms of wujūh al-iḥtijāj (grounds of what is binding), ta'līl (inference) and tarjīḥ (preference) in terms of its being connected with the aṣl (Origin). Thus, Sarakhsī gives a greater definiteness to the doctrine of juristic preference which strengthens and establishes its validity.

Keeping this background in mind, we proceed to present the views of various jurists in each school of thought in chronological order as they were developed in the history of Islamic jurisprudence, and show how they relate to Sarakhsī's doctrine of juristic preference and do not refute his position. Here, we shall first outline in general the views of various jurists from each school of thought without expounding on all the terms and concepts related with the aspect of their specific contentions. They will be discussed later when we proceed to present the views of the individual jurists from each school of thought.

THE ḤANAFĪ SCHOOL OF THOUGHT:

Among the representative jurists from the Ḥanafī school of thought, we shall deal in chronological order with Abū Yūsuf (182 A.H./1310 A.D.), Shaybānī (189 A.H./804 A.D.), Pazdawī (482 A.H./1089 A.D.) and Nasafī (688 A.H./1310 A.D.) to show that their views on the doctrine of juristic preference are not yet quite developed and systematized, as they do not address properly the issue of the 'illa (effective reasoning) which the doctrine of juristic preference employs nor do they justify how such an 'illa is connected with the aṣl (Origin).

Abū Yūsuf and Shaybānī, as already discussed in Chapters Two and Five, employ the doctrine of juristic preference as a methodological approach based on ra'y (reasoning) in a very rudimentary form, although Abū Yūsuf can be said to have extended the usual doctrine of qiyās to istiḥsān in the matters concerning the aḥkām al-dunyā (worldly affairs) for regulating the administrative affairs of Muslims with other nations, and Shaybānī sees istiḥsān as that which is preferable to what the usual deduction by the doctrine of qiyās (systematic reasoning) suggests, but he is not able to explain how its ‘illa is connected with the aṣl (Origin). In other words, he does not conceive of the istiḥsān as a separate and different doctrine from the doctrine of systematic reasoning (qiyās).

Abū al Yūsr al-Pazdawī (482 A.H./1089 A.D.) makes every effort to defend the doctrine of juristic preference against the objections raised by defining and systematizing it to a certain extent. He tries to show that it is not decided by personal inclinations (shahwā) or lack of methodological reasoning; but on the contrary, by purely material considerations provided for in the sharī‘a. ‘Abd Allah ibn Aḥmad al Nasafī (710 A.H./1310 A.D.), basically agrees with the view that the ‘illa used in the doctrine of juristic preference is valid, but shows some concerns as to its being certain (qaṭ‘ī).

THE MĀLIKĪ SCHOOL OF THOUGHT:

Shihāb al-Dīn al Qarāfī (684 A.H./1285 A.D.) and Shāṭibī (790 A.H./1388 A.D) can be described as among those who deal with the systematization of the doctrine of istiṣlāḥ (consideration of what is beneficial or expedient) based on the methodological approach by reasoning (ra᾽y). On the one hand, Qarāfī follows the philosophical position maintained by Rāzī (606 A.H./1209 A.D.), who belongs to the Shāfi‘ī school of thought and, on the other, tries to reconcile it with the doctrine of the Mālikī school of thought. Although according to Qarāfī, maṣlaḥa (what is beneficial or expedient) cannot become the basis of legal reasoning, he recognizes that it can be extended in the cases of prohibitions (ibāḥā) and maṣlaḥa al-mursala (what is neither acknowledged by the sharī‘a nor is considered as ilghā᾽, viz., null and void). Shāṭibī is the only one to extend maṣlaḥa (what is beneficial or expedient) and follows Ghazālī, who represents the Shāfi‘ī school of thought in his concept of maṣlaḥa based on necessity (ḍarūra). Shāṭibi expands the concept of ḍarūra (necessity) by introducing some new elements to be included under it which have not been taken into account by Ghazālī. ‘Abd al-Salām al-Sulmī (600 A.H./1263 A.D.) recognizes the employment of maṣāliḥ al-dunyā (what is beneficial or expedient concerning the worldly affairs) which are based on necessity, but does not contribute much by introducing anything of great significance.

SHĀFI'Ī SCHOOL OF THOUGHT:

In the Shāfi'ī school of thought, the concept of maṣlaḥa (what is beneficial or expedient) as introduced and established by Ghazālī (505 A.H./1111 A.D.), becomes the prominent feature. Provisionally, we shall here introduce how the maṣlaḥa is defined in general and briefly describe other neighboring concepts which were further developed by the individual jurists of the Shāfi'ī school of thought. Basically, maṣlaḥa is defined as that which is beneficial and expedient and is allowed to be used as an 'illa (effective reasoning) to ease the requirements of the Qur'ān and Sunna in case of absolute necessity (ḍarūra), provided it is to promote a presumed general purpose of law and is certain (qaṭ'ī); and is regulated when it is found suitable (munāsab) on the basis of indication (amāra) within the Text to be connected with the command (ḥukm) as we shall discuss later. Here, we need to point out that, as already mentioned, the controversy with regard to the validity of ra'y (reasoning) was reduced to the doctrine of istiḥsān and the doctrine of istiṣlāḥ and now finally it becomes further focused and more narrowed down into the concept of munāsib (what is suitable), that is, if a maṣlaḥa as a munāsaba (suitability or affinity) employed as an 'illa in the doctrine of istiṣlāḥ or what it amounts to in the doctrine of istiḥsān is whether the 'illa is connected with the aṣl (Origin). As a consequence, in the Mālikī school of thought, it is only the maṣlaḥa al-mursala (the maṣlaḥa not supported by the Text) and also the doctrine of istiḥsān which become questionable and controversial. Thereby, other neighboring concepts surface and the concept of maṣlaḥa becomes further refined and developed by the assimilation and integration of the concept of waṣf (characteristic or quality) which limits the derivation of an independent judgment in the legal matters by restricting (takhṣīṣ) it with the sameness of judgments or commands (jins al-aḥkām) and the sameness of things (jinsīya). For example, if the case deals with the derivation of any independent judgment in the matters of prayer, then that judgment should relate with the judgments in the category of prayer and if the judgment is to be derived with regard to an object, then the judgment should relate with the other objects which fall under the same category. These aspects of the concept of maṣlaḥa shall be discussed as we proceed to deal with individual jurists of each school of thought.

Following Ghazālī is Fakhr al-dīn Rāzī (606 A.H./1209 A.D.), whose approach is broader and more philosophical in nature rather than juristic. Nevertheless, Rāzī defines Ghazālī's concept of maṣlaḥa in terms of 'illa (effective reasoning) and identifies it with munāsaba (suitability or affinity). With Isnawī (771 A.H./1370 A.D.), we find that he makes the distinction between jins al-maṣlaḥa (sameness of what is beneficial and expedient) and jins al-aḥkām (sameness of judgments) and restricts ʻilla (effective reasoning) to the jins al-aḥkām only. Ibn Taymīya (728-A.H./1326 A.D.) introduces the concept of takhṣīṣ al-ʻilla (restriction or particularization of effective reasoning) based on the notion of the maʻānī (inward meaning) and favors it by calling it the qiyās al-mʻānawī (systematic reasoning based on the inward meaning) as seen in his treatise on **Istiḥsān**. From this, his position emerges wherein the munāsaba is viewed as having the waṣf (characteristic or quality) of jins al-aḥkām (sameness of judgments) based on naṣṣ (textual evidence on the basis of Qurʾān and Sunna) and ijmāʻ (general consensus) in the ḥukm (command) under consideration. But, on the whole, as he appears to state in his treatise on **Istiḥsān**, he favors the doctrine of istiḥsān and holds it to be valid. Tāj al-Dīn Subkī (771 A.H./1369 A.D.), combines his position with Ghazālī and Rāzī. Broadly speaking, Subkī introduces that the waṣf (characteristic or quality) of munāsaba (suitability or affinity) of maṣlaḥa (what is beneficial or expedient) to be used as an ʻilla (effective reasoning) in a command (ḥukm) should be related with the aṣl (Origin) and discusses further how the shurūṭ (conditions) in the forms of the jinsīya (sameness of things), istithnāʾ (exception), istidrāk (rectification) and munāqidha (opposite) are employed in the maṣlaḥa. Masʻūd Ibn ʻOmar al-Taftāzānī (792 A.H./1414 A.D.) considers that the waṣf (characteristic or quality) of the ʻilla (effective reasoning) in the doctrine of juristic preference is not that of the qiyās and what the upholders of the doctrine of juristic preference claim that its ʻilla is strong, is simply ẓann (speculation). Moreover, the ʻilla as they employ in the doctrine of juristic preference does not adhere to the wordings and figurative application, and also, that in the exercise of the doctrine of juristic preference one wujh al-iḥtijāj (ground of what is binding) is emphasized over the other wujūh al-iḥtijāj (grounds of what is binding).

ḤAMBALĪ SCHOOL OF THOUGHT:

In the Ḥambalī school of thought, we shall deal with Ibn Ḥazm (456 A.H./1064 A.D.), who actually belongs to the Ẓāhirīya school of thought which tries to lean heavily on aḥādith (traditions) and, as already mentioned, does away with any kind of raʾy (reasoning). Ibn Ḥazm rejects istiḥsān (doctrine of juristic preference) outright without even dealing with the issue regarding the ʻilla (effective reasoning) which is employed in the doctrine of istiḥsān. Ṭūfī (716 A.H./1316 A.D.), as well as Rashīd Riḍā (1243 A.H./1865 A.D) who was an independent thinker of his time rather than strictly speaking a follower of his own former Ḥambalī school of thought, are of great importance as they both, once again, focus on the maṣlaḥa and the istiḥsān and examine the validity of 'illa employed in these doctrines.

Section III: VIEWS AND OBJECTIONS RAISED BY THE INDIVIDUAL JURISTS FROM THE FOUR SCHOOLS OF THOUGHT AGAINST RA'Y IN THE FORM OF THE DOCTRINE OF ISTIḤSĀN (JURISTIC PREFERENCE) AND THE DOCTRINE OF ISTIṢLĀḤ (CONSIDERATION OF WHAT IS BENEFICIAL AND EXPEDIENT) IN RELATION TO SARAKHSĪ'S POSITION

We shall now proceed to present, in chronological order, the views of individual jurists from each school of thought concerning the 'illa employed in the exercise of ra'y as a juristic methodological approach in the form of the doctrine of istiḥsān (juristic preference) and the doctrine of istiṣlāḥ (consideration of what is beneficial and expedient) and show specifically how the objections raised by these individual jurists do not refute Sarakhsī's position.

THE INDIVIDUAL JURISTS FROM THE ḤANAFĪ SCHOOL OF THOUGHT:

We shall first deal with the views of Abū al-Yūsar al-Pazdawī (482 A.H./1089 A.D.) from his **Uṣūl** as commented by 'Abd al-'Azīz bin Aḥmad al-Bukhārī (730 A.H./1329 A.D.). In the first place, Pazdawī defends Abū Ḥanīfa's position concerning the istiḥsān (doctrine of juristic preference) and says that some false accusers have attacked Abū Ḥanīfa and his followers for abandoning the doctrine of qiyās (systematic reasoning) in favor of the doctrine of istiḥsān (juristic preference). They maintain that only the Qur'ān, Sunna, ijma' and qiyās can be the sources for the athar (evidence) and the doctrine of istiḥsān (juristic preference) is the fifth principle recognized by Abū Ḥanīfa alone.[12] Shāfi'ī further exaggerated this in his refutation of the doctrine of istiḥsān, for he said, "whoever does the exercise of istiḥsān places himself in the place of God as a legislator."[13] According to Pazdawī, this accusation is unexamined and not well founded. In fact, the opponents have not blamed Abū Ḥanīfa for the istiḥsān whose 'illa is based on athar (evidence) from the Sunna, ijmā' or ḍarūra (necessity), as the ḍarūra for the abandonment of the qiyās in favor of the istiḥsān is granted on these grounds anonymously by all; rather, what they have blamed him for is professing that the istiḥsān is based on individual opinion. But that is not true since, according to us (namely, the Ḥanafī school of thought), the istiḥsān is only one kind of qiyās and is not simply invented by way of passion (shahwā) and without any evidence. At this point, as commented by Bukhārī, Pazdawī cites the opinion of Karkhī (340 A.H./951 A.D.) that in case of some legal problem, the exception is created from its analogous precedent on the basis of some stronger evidence which renders it distinguishable.[14] Thus, when two qiyās oppose one another or are different from one another, one of them is preferred and the qiyās which is preferred is called the istiḥsān in order to indicate that it is stronger than the other qiyās.[15] Hence, from the very beginning, Pazdawī clarifies the validity of istiḥsān by stating in his discussion that he does not intend to divide the qiyās and the istiḥsān into two separate categories as if they are different from one another. Likewise, the istiḥsān which is established by the naṣṣ (textual evidence), ijmā' (general consensus) and ḍarūra (necessity) is not being excluded in the exercise of ijtiḥād (exercise of deriving independent legal judgment based on the four sources of Islamic jurisprudence),[16] since the istiḥsān is not different from the qiyās and is not exercised except when it fulfills the conditions which are also necessary for the qiyās.[17]

Thus, Pazdawī makes the distinction between the qiyās and the istiḥsān which lies only in the different kind of 'illa they employ. In the qiyās, the 'illa is ẓāhir (apparent) but it is weak (ḍa'īf), in the istiḥsān, although the 'illa is khafī (concealed), it is strong (qawī) and thus the justification for employing the latter. This is, he argues, based on the notion of ma'ānī (inward meaning) to be employed in the istiḥsān of what the qiyās formally intends to achieve. One can notice that Pazdawī is in agreement with Sarakhsī in his interpretation of 'illa as being concealed, but strong and, therefore, it is justified to use it in the doctrine of istiḥsān as against the doctrine of qiyās, the 'illa of which, although apparent, is weak. Nonethless, Pazdawī yet falls short of what follows from the juxtaposition of the doctrine of istiḥsān with the subject matter of muwāda'a (treaties) and mu'āmalāt (mutual relations) concerning the aḥkām al-dunyā (worldly affairs) which takes into account the material facts to be encompassed under the sharī'a law. This is because Pazdawī still argues for the validity of istiḥsān within the aḥkām al-dīn (religious affairs) in constrast to Sarakhsī, who finds the relevance of the doctrine of istiḥsān not only within the aḥkām al-dīn (religious affairs), but also more importantly in the matters of muwāda'a (treaties) and mu'āmlāt (mutual relations) of Muslims with other nations concerning the aḥkām al-dunyā (worldly affairs).

'Abd Allah ibn Aḥmad al-Nasafī (710 A.H./1310 A.D.) regarding the 'illa used in the doctrine of istiḥsān basically asserts the view that it is based on the athar (evidence), ijmā' (general consensus) and ḍarūra (necessity) and states that it is based on the 'illa (effective reasoning) or athar (evidence) which is khafī (concealed) in the istiḥsān and is perfectly acceptable, if it is obviously not harmful and has a stronger 'illa.

But, al-Nasafī shows some reservations and draws attention toward the aspect of its being certain (qaṭ'ī) or not. First, the 'illa to be connected with the aṣl (Origin) could itself be wrong,[18] or the conditions wherein the 'illa may have been used is in exactly the opposite manner than it should have been,[19] or the sabab (reason or motive) which leads to the ḥukm (judgment) is such that no one in his right mind agrees with it.[20] It is also possible that any other waṣf (characteristic or quality) could have been connected as an 'illa with the aṣl (Origin) rather than the one which is employed by the istiḥsān in the ḥukm (judgment) under consideration.[21] Again, it is possible that from the very beginning one has connected the 'illa to the aṣl (Origin) in a mistaken way; then obviously it stands in the way concerning the ḥukm (judgment) under consideration, so far as its suitability or affintiy (munāsaba) is concerned.[22] It is also possible that the one who exercises the istiḥsān changes his position regarding that particular 'illa he has employed and later comes to think of it not as a proper 'illa.[23]

These reservations shown by al-Nasafī are, no doubt, quite important as far as the application of the istiḥsān is concerned. They are practical concerns and subject to the process of trial and error. But, so far as Sarakhsī's position is concerned, the theoretical basis of the istiḥsān in principle remains unchanged, and muchless, the validity of the doctrine as such.

THE INDIVIDUAL JURISTS FROM THE SHĀFI'Ī SCHOOL OF THOUGHT:

The controversy in the historical development of Islamic jurisprudence regarding the doctrine of istiḥsān as a methodological juristic reasoning begins first with the Mu'atazilī Abū al-Ḥusayn al-Baṣrī (436 A.H./1044 A.D.). It is difficult to say with certainty that Baṣrī belongs to the Ḥanafī or the Shāfi'ī school of thought. It is maintained that because the Ḥanafī Qāḍī Abū 'Abd Allah al-Ṣamārī led the funeral prayer for al-Baṣrī, he should have belonged to the Ḥanafī school of thought, and not to the Shafi'ī.[24] Whatever may be the case, he is critical of the doctrine of istiḥsān and his objections against the validity of the 'illa of the doctrine of istiḥsān are in agreement with the position maintained by the Shāfi'ī school of thought.

Baṣrī's criticism centers around three specific points: the first deals with the istiḥsān itself as a form of ijtihād (exercise of deriving an independent judgment in the legal matters based on the four sources of Islamic jurisprudence) and the other two deal with the 'illa of the doctrine of istiḥsān.

According to Baṣrī, when the upholders of the doctrine of istiḥsān assert that the evidence (athar) on the basis of which the change is made in the ḥukm (judgment) by abandoning the qiyās in favor of the isthṣān, then we know exactly that it is based on passion (shahwā) or inclination (khāṭir) or the indications (amāra) founded by the ẓann (speculation). In such cases, it would not be possible to distinguish between what is valid and what is invalid.[25]

The Ḥanafī jurists try to explain that the istiḥsān is based on the notion of ma'ānī (inward meaning) and hold that some indications (amāra) are stronger than the others and, thereby, claim that in the exercise of istiḥsān, one uses the stronger evidence and they refer to it as the takhṣīṣ (particularization or restriction) on the basis of which they insist on abandoning the qiyās in favor of the istiḥsān. According to Baṣrī, this kind of istiḥsān is invalid, since a change can occur in the ḥukm (judgment) not based on the naṣṣ (textual evidence).[26] Other upholders of the doctrine of istiḥsān argue for the takhṣīṣ (particularization or restriction) by the dalīl (evidence) which is stronger. But, this kind of istiḥsān is also not valid because there is an abandonment of qiyās which is generally accepted and that leaves aside an account to be given as to what is held as valid in the other aḥkām (judgments) which are already established on the basis of qiyās.[27]

Finally, in the exercise of istiḥsān one omits a wide range of wujūh (grounds) of what is binding which are inclusive in the qiyās at the cost of emphasizing only one specific wujh (ground) of what is binding. According to Baṣrī, this is extraneous to the judgment or to the aṣl (Origin) and is not the condition for exercising the ijtihād (deriving an independent judgment or ḥukm in legal matters based on the four sources of Islamic jurisprudence). It is ẓann (speculation) on the part of those who exercise istiḥsān, even if the one who uses it terms it as the istiḥsān.[28]

From this it can be discerned that Baṣrī's criticism of the doctrine of istiḥsān is not valid as we have shown that Sarakhsī in his **Mabsūṭ** tries in anticipation of such criticisms to base the 'illa of the doctrine of istiḥsān as being directly derived from the Qur'ān, and aḥadīth (traditions) and, furthermore, in his **Uṣūl al-Fiqh**, Sarakhsī follows the conditions for its employment as they are observed in the doctrine of qiyās. Other objections raised by Baṣrī will be answered as we proceed in the course of our discussion.

Abū Ḥāmid Muḥammad al-Ghazālī (505 A.H./1111 A.D.) in his discussion of the validity of 'illa employed in the juristic methodological reasoning identifies in some ways the istiḥsān with the istiṣlāḥ (to decide in favor of something because it is considered good, namely the maṣlaḥa) or maṣlaḥa al-mursala (the maṣlaḥa not explicitly supported by the Text i.e., the Qur'ān or Sunna), although maintaining a very important and fine distinction between the two doctrines. At this point only those aspects of Ghazālī's thoughts are introduced which are directly related to the maṣlaḥa al-mursala and the istiḥsān. Other important aspects of his thoughts shall be discussed when we come to deal with Subkī, who essentially follows Ghazālī's position by refining and modifying it further.

According to Ghazālī, the maṣlaḥa al-mursala is accepted both by Abū Ḥanīfa and Mālik and is rejected by Shāfi'ī. Ghazālī asserts that both the istiṣlāḥ and the istiḥsān are methods of reasoning which do not have the same validity that the doctrine of qiyās has. Ghazālī expounds on the notion of ijtihād (deriving an independent judgment in legal matters on the basis of the four sources of Islamic jurisprudence) in his **Mustaṣfā** at great length and with detailed examples.[29] He establishes here that if valid qiyās is to be exercised, it is to be limited to the strict 'illa; otherwise, it is uṣūl mahūma (the principles on which the one who does derive the indepedent judgment in legal matters based on the four sources of Islamic jurisprudence relies on imagination or on individual discretion). However, Ghazālī approves of the maṣlaḥa only when: (i) it is ḍarūrī (necessary), because it consists of preserving one of the five necessary principles, i.e., protection of religion, life, reason, progeny and property; (ii) it is qaṭ'ī (certain), because it is definitely known that this way the lives of the Muslim communtiy will be safe; (iii) it is kullī (collectively whole), because it takes into consideration collectively the whole community and not a part of it (juz'ī).[30]

But, Ghazālī rejects the istiḥsān, since he considers that it is entirely based on individual discretion rather than on the basis of evidence wherein the 'illa sought is naqlīya (traditional, i.e., based on the four sources of Islamic jurisprudence).[31] This is brought out by Ghazālī while discussing the doctrine of qiyās. According to Ghazālī, qiyās has four components: (i) aṣl, the Origin or root from which the systematic reasoning is made; (ii) far', the branch (of law) for which the systematic reasoning is exercised (iii) 'illa, the effective reasoning on the basis of which systematic reasoning is exercised; (iv) the ḥukm (judgment) to which the exercise of systematic reasoning leads.

Now, according to Ghazālī, the 'illa is (i) either explicit (ṣarīḥ) or (ii) it is implicitly indicated (imā'), or (iii) it is known from the sequence and order (sabab wa tartīb) of the command, or (iv) finding out the 'illa by instinbāṭ (inference). There are two valid methods of instinbāṭ by which the 'illa can be determined and deduced: (i) al-sabr wa al-taqsīim (observation and classification) and munāsaba (suitability or affinity). Ghazālī defines the munāsaba as that which, like maṣlaḥa, becomes regulated (and is rationally achieved) as soon as it is connected with the aṣl (Origin)

However, as Masud quite appropriately observes, the munāsaba and maṣlaḥa are not identical. Among the various classifications of munāsib, one is of particular significance to us, as it explains the relationship of munāsib to maṣlaḥa and is the central difference of opinion between the Ḥanafī school of thought and the Mālīkī as well as the Shāfi'ī schools of thought. As the question regarding the validity of ra'y became reduced and accentuated in the doctrines of istiḥsān and istiṣlaḥ, now the question regarding the 'illa they both employ becomes further narrowed down, properly focused on the concept of munāsib (suitability or affinity) as introduced by Ghazālī. This becomes clear with Ghazālī's classification of various munāsib (what is suitable) into four categories:

First, the munāsib which is suitable to and supported by a specific textual evidence. Second, the munāsib which is neither suitable to nor supported by the textual evidence. Third, the munāsib which is not suitable to but is supported by the textual evidence. Fourth, the munāsib which is suitable to but not supported by the textual evidence.[32]

According to Ghazālī, the first category is accepted by all jurists. The second category is called the istiḥsān which clearly means "to make law according to personal discretion." The third and fourth are called the istiṣlāḥ or istidlāl al-mursal.

It is evident from this classification that the maṣlaḥa is the basic consideration for deciding the suitability or munāsaba of something which the istiḥān lacks.[33] Ghazālī approves of the maṣlaḥa or istiṣlāḥ with reluctancy but rejects the istiḥsān outright. In fact, at one place in his **Mustaṣfā**, he remarks that "whoever does exercise the istiṣlāḥ, he does legislate the sharī'a law, as in the case of one who does exercise istiḥsān." [34] Thus, it was this kind of munāsib (suitability or affinity) associated with the doctrine of istiḥsān which became increasingly the subject of controversy among the jurists from the Shāfi'ī and Mālikī schools of thought.

It becomes clear from the above discussion that, in the first place, Ghazālī sees the doctrines of istiṣlāḥ and istiḥsān mainly in the context of aḥkām al-dīn (religious affairs) and, more importantly in the second place, Sarakhsī in his systematization of the doctrine of juristic preference restrospectively and as well in anticipation takes into consideration all these aspects and objections and examines the 'illa of the doctrine of juristic preference as being connected with the aṣl (Origin) not only in the matters concerning the aḥkām al-dīn (religious affairs), but also in juxtaposition with the subject matter of muwāda'a (treaties) and mu'āmalāt (mutual relations) concerning the aḥkām al-dunyā (worldly affairs).

Following Ghazālī is Fakhr al-Dīn al-Rāzī (606 A.H./1209), who discusses maṣlaḥa al-mursala (a maṣlaḥa not explicitly supported by the amā' i.e., indication from the Text). Rāzī's approach toward the issue is rather philosophical and not quite juristic and is in reference to Mu'tazilites who believe that God is obligated to consider maṣlaḥa.[35] He does not focus directly on the controversial aspect of the validity of 'illa in the maṣlaḥa al-mursala and hurriedly disposes of the istiḥsān as being invalid without examining it. Therefore, it would suffice for our purpose to state his position in general. He interprets the ḥikām (wisdom) and the maṣāliḥ (plural of maṣlaḥa) as the causes or motives of God's commands. With Rāzī, the munāsaba and maṣlaḥa become closely associated with each other. The munāsaba is explained as being an 'illa. He argues that to prove the munāsab can be an 'illa, there are three premises to be established. First, God issued the commands for the maṣāliḥ of the people. Second, the case under consideration consists of the maṣlaḥa. Third, it can be shown that the probable reason for God's issuing that particular command is this particular maṣlaḥa.[36] According to Rāzī, when we observe the sharī'a, we find that the commands and maṣāliḥ occur together without being separated from each other and this is known inductively.[37] As opposed to what the Mu'tazalites maintain, Rāzī stresses that no motive or cause can be attributed to God's command or acts, yet, according to Rāzī, God's commands are for the maṣlaḥa of the people and this maṣlaḥa or munāsaba can be considered as an 'illa for the command. Thus, Rāzī's point of view as discussed is of a very general philosophical nature which does not address specifically the issue of the validity of 'illa for its employment in the maṣlaḥa mursala or istiḥsān. It is not certain as Isnawī observes, if Rāzī on this particular issue agrees with other jurists as to its validity.[38]

Next to follow is Jamāl al-Dīn al Isnawī (771 A.H./1370 A.D.), who combines Ghazālī's and Rāzī's positions,[39] but he leans heavily on Ghazālī as he states that the maṣlaḥa is permissible only on the ground of five necessities (ḍarūra) quoting Ghazālī verbatim,[40] and argues that if the evidence (dalīl) is not given, its absence is assumed, thereby, forcing us to assume that there is no ḥukm (judgment), as the evidence is not connected with the aṣl (Origin) in the ḥukm (judgment).[41] This is the position he claims to support from Rāzī's **Maḥṣūl**, as he remarks in the same vein that Rāzī considers it to be the standpoint of some jurists, but does not clarify if he (Rāzī) agrees with them.[42]

Isnawī further specifies that when the maṣlaḥa is employed, it should be the maṣlaḥa kullīya (what is beneficial or expedient for the whole community) and not simply the maṣlaḥa juz'ī (for part of it).[43] Isnawī also rejects the jins al-maṣlaḥa (sameness of maṣlaḥa), which according to him is considered ẓann (speculation) in contrast to what is qiyās, which is solely based on the jins al-aḥkām (sameness of judgments),[44] as there would be no valid istidlāl (evidence) on the basis of which the ḥukm (judgment) is connected with the aṣl (Origin). This he explains with the example of grapes, and the laws regarding it are now applied to the raisins in the contract of sale, and the istidlāl (evidence) which was valid in the case of grapes, is now applied as an istidlāl (evidence) in the ḥukm (judgment) regarding the case of raisins. Here, the jin al-aḥkām (sameness of judgments) is simply lacking. According to Isnawī, such a kind of istidlāl (evidence) is sheer speculation (ẓann) on the part of the one who exercises it, because to begin with there is no ḥukm (judgment) regarding that particular thing (jins) under consideration to which the evidence is connected and on the basis of which the qiyās is exercised. On the whole, Isnawī concludes by maintaining that in the exercise of istiḥsān, there is no evidence (istidlāl) found for a ḥukm (judgment) as based on the stronger evidence (istidlāl) claimed by the upholders of the doctrine of istiḥsān which forces us to abandon the qiyās.[45]

From this one can see that Isnawī introduces the maṣlaḥa kullīya (what is beneficial or expedient for the whole community) and the jins al-aḥkām as the necessary conditions to exercise the qiyās and limits the use of raʾy (reasoning) by restricting (takhṣīṣ) the 'illa to be more focused, determined and specified. To address this concern of Isnawī in relevance to Sarakhsī's position regarding the doctrine of istiḥsān, it can be said: First, Sarakhsī has taken into account the aspect of jins al-aḥkām in the systematization of his doctrine of istiḥsān; and, to be more specific, his analysis of the case of a donation (ṣadaqa), as already discussed in Chapter Four, suffices to clarify that such donations should be accompanied by the condition of intention for the specific kind of donation. If one gives a donation (ṣadaqa) but not intending it as an alms tax (zakāt), it should be considered as the ṣadaqa (donation) and not the alms tax (zakāt).[46] Second, Sarakhsī's doctrine of istiḥsān does not only deal with the aḥkām al-dīn (religious affairs) but it also deals with the wider and broader issues in the matters of muwāda'a (treaties) and mu'āmalāt (mutual relations) concerning the aḥkām al-dunyā (worldly affairs) and, naturally, such matters as the welfare and interests of the whole community are of first and foremost consideration, as already shown in Chapters Two and Five when we disussed the ḥāja or ḍarūra (necessity) as a constitutive element and material fact which takes into account such factors in the subject matter of muwāda'a (treaties) and mu'āmalāt (mutual relations).

Tāj al-Dīn al-Subkī (771 A.H./1369 A.D.) also combines Ghazālī and Rāzī, but tries to be more systematic and specific in his analysis of 'illa which is to be connected with the aṣl (Origin). He analyzes the waṣf (characteristic or quality) and the munāsaba (suitability or affinity) and tries to establish that they as the 'illa should be connected with the aṣl (Origin), otherwise they are properly considered not as the 'illa for their use in the sharī'a and categorically cannot be used in the 'ibādāt (religious observances).

In the section "Masālik al-'Illa" (Procedures for Deducing 'Illa) of his **Jāmi' al-Jawāmi'**, Subkī sets out the conditions which an 'illa should meet in order that it can be used in the ḥukm (judgment). It is either accepted by the ijmā' (general consensus), or it is based on an explicit textual evidence (naṣṣ ṣarīḥ)[47] or where the imā' (implicit indication) is linked to the waṣf (characteristic or quality) by the wordings and the ḥukm (judgment) is derived on that ground, or where the sameness of waṣf is found in the ḥukm (judgment).[48] Subkī explains the last two cases with examples, after the narration from al-A'rābī. The Prophet was asked: "I slept with my wife during the daytime in the month of Ramḍān, what should I do?" He was told to free a slave. This occurrence gives an implicit indication for the 'illa; otherwise, the question could not have been answered in this manner. But, "never make a decision in the state of anger", the prohibition of making a decision is seen as an explicit indication, because when one is angry, one loses his mind. Thus, the distinction between the two cases consists in that in the first case, the implicit indication, as described, is accompanied by the wordings in the ḥukm (judgment), while in the second case, the explicit indication for the ḥukm (judgment) is provided.

Subkī further discusses how the stipulations (shurūṭ) made in certain judgments can be used as the 'illa in other judgments:

(i) Gold for gold, silver for silver etc., mithl bi mithl (same for the same). The jinsīya (sameness of the thing) as stipulated in one judgment can be used as an 'illa in other judgments.
(ii) In the cases of ilghā' (what is declared as invalid), for example, "do not approach them (women) until they are clean. But when they have purified themselves, you may approach them."[49] Here, the 'illa is based on the prohibition in the ḥukm (judgment) to approach women while they are menstruating, and the permissibility when they are not menstruating.
(iii) The cases of istithnā' (exception), for example, "the half of the dowry is due to them (men), unless they (women) forgive it." Here, the 'illa in the ḥukm (judgment) for being forgiven is based on the exception (istithnā').

(iv) The case of istidrāk (rectification), for example, "God will not call you to account for thoughtlessness in your oaths, but for the intentions in your hearts." The distinction between the two judgments lies in the istidrāk (rectification) that in the first case God will forgive you, but will not in the second case.[50]

In the above examples as analyzed by Subkī, it is shown that the 'illa is accompanied by the ḥukm (judgment).

Now, we come to deal with the concept of tartīb al-ḥukm (order of the command) on the basis of the waṣf (characteristic or quality). According to Subkī, if it was not an 'illa, it is impossible that the learned jurists would have used it in the juristic methodology of reasoning. Thus, in the cases of ḥukm (judgment) dealing with the prohibitions, it will be nullified by what is required, such as in the case of "hasten earnestly to the remembrance of God and leave off business."[51] The implication is that when one is busy in trading, he might miss the prayer and that is the implicit indication which becomes waṣf (characteristic or quality) in the ḥukm (judgment) by the wordings. To say it more correctly, here the implicit indication is necessary for the ḥukm (judgment) to have the specific waṣf (characteristic or quality), contrary to the cases which permit the waṣf (characteristic or quality) to be of a more general nature such as in the case of "God has permitted one to trade."

In al-sabr wa al-taqsīm (the observation and classification, the method of exclusion), one observes the auṣāf (plural of waṣf) as belonging together in a given object on the basis of which the aṣl (Origin) is formed and assigns them as belonging to it and rejects the other remaining auṣāf (characteriastics or qualities) not found in it, and, thereby considers them as not belonging to it. For example, there are auṣāf pertaining to one commodity such as maize and one observes them if they are found in another commodity, such as wheat, then one might be able to restrain (ḥaṣr) to observation only. If the restraining (ḥaṣr) and rejecting of auṣāf is found certain (qaṭ'ī), then the ḥukm (judgment) based on it is considered as being certain (qaṭī). In cases wherein the restraining and rejecting or excluding of auṣāf (characteristics or qualities) are ẓannī (speculative) and they are compared with other cases wherein they are qaṭ'ī (certain), then the ḥukm (judgment) made on that basis is considered as being ẓannī (speculative) rather than qaṭ'ī.[52]

Seemingly quite aware of the contention of the Ḥanafī school of thought regarding the issue of 'illa as its being apparent (ẓāhir) or concealed (khafī or bāṭin), Subkī maintains that in the maṣlaḥa, whether the waṣf (characteristic or quality) is ẓāhir (apparent) or concealed (khafī), the ḥukm (judgment) is to be based on the aṣl (Origin), otherwise it is not considered as qaṭ'ī (certain). As an example, Subkī discusses the case of tarkhkhuṣ (concessions) in fasting (ṣaum) during a journey. Here, Subkī argues that in this case, the ta'līl (inference) is to be regarded as being ẓannī (speculative), since the ta'līl (inference) for the tarkhkhuṣ (concessions) can vary from person to person, time to time and circumstance to circumstance.[53]

Regarding the munāsaba, if it carries the sameness of characteristics or qualities (jins al-auṣāf) and the sameness of judgments (jins al-aḥkām) in the given ḥukm (judgment) on the basis of naṣṣ (textual evidence) and ijmā' (general consensus), it is accepted as effective (mu'ththir) and also considered as being effective (mu'ththir) as the ta'līl (inference), if it carries the tartīb (order) of the ḥukm in accordance with the waṣf.[54]

With this, Subkī comes to define the maṣlaḥa and concludes that if the waṣf is not munāsab on the above grounds and the evidence is established to cancel it, it is not to be used as an 'illa. But when the evidence neither cancels it nor establishes it, it is considered as the maṣlaḥa al-mursala and is accepted by Mālik. According to Subkī, it is to be rejected, especially where the 'ibādāt (religious observances) are concerned, as the maṣāliḥ in the 'ibādāt should be ḍarūrī (necessary), qaṭ'ī (certain) and kullī (for the whole community).[55]

With Subkī, the discussion regarding maṣlaḥa on the formal doctrinal level of istiṣlāḥ reaches its climax in this school of thought, though materially not yet as enriched as what we shall find later with Shāṭibī. Here on the doctrinal level, one can say that the culmination of Subkī's doctrine of maṣlaḥa as a juristic methodology of legal reasoning comes very close to Sarakhsī's doctrine of istiḥsān wherein Sarakhsī analyzes all the aspects of 'illa as used in the various forms of the doctrine of istiḥsān and shows that it is based on and connected with the aṣl (Origin). Thus, as a conclusion, Sarakhsī is able to state all the conditions which the doctrine of istiḥsān should meet in order to be employed as a valid legal methodological reasoning within the sharī'a law. Subkī, in his doctrine of istiṣlāḥ, employs the maṣlaḥa, like Sarakhsī does with the 'illa in the doctrine of istiḥsān in terms of its being related to and determined as the munāsaba (suitability or affinity) to the aṣl (Origin). He further specifies in the doctrine of istiṣlāḥ, like Sarakhsī does in his doctrine of istiḥsān, that in any ḥukm (judgment) under consideration the 'illa used by it should strictly meet the condition of the jins al-aḥkām (sameness of the judgments) and the sameness of objects,[56] so that the specificity of 'illa employed in the ḥukm (judgment) approximates completely and in the same manner with the 'illa of the jins al-aḥkām (sameness of judgments) with the jinsīya (sameness of objects) which Sarakhsī also specifies in his analysis of the doctrine of istiḥsān as already discussed and shown in Chapter Five.

The only difference between Subkī's doctrine of istiṣlāḥ and Sarakhsī's doctrine of istiḥsān lies in the fact that Subkī, like all other Mālikī jurists in general, attempts to make the doctrine of istiṣlāḥ valid as a methodological juristic reasoning, but confined unlike Sarakhsī, only to the aḥkām al-dīn (religious affairs); and, thereby, the material facts which enter into consideration in the contents of muwāda'a (treaties) and mu'āmlāt (mutual relations) concerning the aḥkām al-dunyā (worldly affairs) are not addressed and subjected on any definite doctrinal basis as does Sarakhsī by his doctrine of juristic preference.

Aḥmad 'Abd al-Ḥalīm Ibn Taymīya (728 A.H./1328 A.D.) is hesitant to accept the validity of maṣlaḥa al-mursala or istiḥsān and dhawq al-ṣufīya (mystic taste) as seen in his work **Majmū'āt al-Rasā'il wa al-Masā'il**. However, in his treatise on the **Istiḥsān**, which was completed by him but was left in the stage of a rough copy,[57] we find that Ibn Taymīya, in his discussion on the istiḥsān in relation to the qiyās (doctrine of systematic reasoning) and the takhṣīṣ al-'illa (particularization or restriction of 'illa), states that "a sound istiḥsān does not constitute a breach of a sound analogy (qiyās) and that it is not lawful to deviate from a sound analogy in any case whatsoever."[58]

First, we shall deal with Ibn Taymīya's **Majmū'āt al-Rasā'il**, wherein he maintains that the maṣlaḥa is similar to the ra'y and close to the istiḥsān and kashf (mystic revelation) or dhawq al-ṣūfīya (mystic taste).[59] Here, he brings out that the sharī'a as such does not disregard the maṣlaḥa, but then the maṣlaḥa should be based on the evidence from the Qur'ān, Sunna and ijmā' (general consensus), and the maṣlaḥa in no case should be contrary to the sharī'a either by the naṣṣ (textual evidence) or by the doctrine of qiyās (systematic reasoning).[60]

Nevertheless, Ibn Taymīya here concludes that the maṣlaḥa, which he identifies at this point with the istiḥsān or istiṣlāḥ,[61] are not rejected by the sharī'a and are obviously furnished in the Text, that is, the Qur'ān and Ḥadīth. If human reason does not find it as the maṣlaḥa, it is either due to the incapacity of human reason to reach it or it can go astray and mistakenly find something which seems as useful but, in fact, might be harmful. Thus, it is the Text and not the maṣlaḥa or istiḥsān which remains the final authority for legislating any sharī'a law.[62]

However, as already mentioned, Ibn Taymīya in his treaty on the **Istiḥsān** argues for its validity. It is also to be noted that Ibn Taymīya here directs his attention exclusively to the doctrine of istiḥsān by analyzing the 'illa it employs. He discusses the istiḥsān here in relation to the takhṣīṣ al-'illa (particularization or restriction of 'illa) and the basis of the notion of ma'ānī (inward meaning). With this, Ibn Taymīya offers a rebuttal against Shāfi'ī and Mālik who reject the istiḥsān and consider it invalid, because of the change which takes place in the ḥukm (judgment) due to the takhṣīṣ al-'illa (particularization or restriction of 'illa).[63] Ibn Taymīya argues against this and for the appropriateness of istiḥsān by asserting that there is nothing in the sharī'a against the valid qiyās in the form of istiḥsān, which employs the 'illa based on the notion of ma'ānī (inward meaning) by virtue of which the ḥukm (judgment) is established and is considered as valid.[64] He illustrates this on the basis of a narration from Marūdhī who said: it is valid to buy the land not owned by anyone (sawād al-arḍ), but it is not valid to sell it. Thereupon it was asked, "how would it be bought if it is not owned?" He answered: "by qiyās."[65] But, it would be said, as Ibn Taymīya claims, it is the istiḥsān, on the ground that it is allowed to buy the copies of Qur'ān, but not to sell them. This is similar to that case. Here, the qiyās has been exercised in consideration with one special or specific ground (wujh) from among all the wujūh (grounds).[66]

Thus, according to Ibn Taymīya, as seen from his treaty on the **Istiḥsān**, the qiyās as understood is the qiyās al-lafẓī (qiyās based on the wording) as well as the qiyās al-ma'ānawī (qiyās based on the inward meaning), and in both cases it is perfectly valid to employ them in the sharī'a law. Ibn Taymīya is inclined more toward mystical teachings and as such not interested in the juristic details and critical analysis of the 'illa whether employed in the form of the doctrine of qiyās or istiḥsān and even much less interested to see it from the wider perspective of muwāda'a (treaties) and mu'āmalāt (mutual relations) concerning the aḥkām al-dunyā (worldly affairs) as we find with Sarakhsī.

The most thorough and extensive discussion on the issue is to be found with Mas'ūd ibn 'Omar al-Taftāzānī (792 A.H./1414 A.D.) in his **Sharḥ al-Talwīḥ 'alā al-Tawḍīḥ**. Taftāzānī combines his position with Rāzī,but with a difference of great importance. He approaches the issue directly, addressing how human reason ('aql) does not establish the 'illa necessary for the validity of istiḥsān or maṣlaḥa, whereas Rāzī leaves it unexplained, if not quite unanswered. Taftāzānī comes to hold the same position as did Rāzī, but in order to establish his standpoint, Taftāzānī tries to show by employing Baṣrī, Ghazālī and others that the 'illa as employed in the doctrine of istiḥsān is not valid. Taftāzānī claims that the 'illa, professed by the upholders of the doctrine of istiḥsān as being qawī (strong) though khafī (concealed) and on the basis of which the validity is given to the 'illa of the doctrine does not have the waṣf (characteristic or quality) which is necessary for exercising any valid ijtihād (the derivation of an independent judgment in the legal matters on the basis of the four sources of Islamic jurisprudence), and the claim of its validity on the basis of the notion of ma'ānī (inward meaning) is the discretion on the part of the one who exercises the ijtihād, and hence, it is not considered as being qaṭ'ī (certain). His basic position is that all aḥkām (judgments) derived from the sharī'a sources are qaṭ'ī (certain) and they remain the same before or after the ijtihād (derivation of an indepedent judgment in the legal matters based on the four sources of Islamic jurisprudence) has been exercised.[67] In the ijtihād, one connects the 'illa with the aṣl (Origin) and if not, it is considered simply ẓann (speculation) and, thus, not qaṭ'ī (certain). It is either bāṭil (invalid) or fāsid (false).[68] He strives to demonstrate this at great length.

Taftāzānī first analyzes the notion of ta'līl (determination of the sabab, namely, cause or reason of the command by logical deduction or inference). It is obvious that the sabab (cause or reason) is used in the sense of 'illa (effective reasoning) on the basis of which logical deduction or inference is made. Taftāzānī sets out four conditions required for the valid ta'līl (inference) in any qiyās without explaining them explicitly. These four conditions are as follows:

The first condition is the establishment of sabab (cause or reason) and the waṣf (characteristic or quality) of it. The second condition is the establishment of the shart (condition) or wasf in a hukm (judgment) in such a way that the condition of sameness of the judgments (ahkām) and the sameness of objects (jinsīya) is established and the wasf becomes determined. The third condition is the establishment of hukm or wasf, namely, with the determination of wasf in the case of any hukm (judgment) under consideration, it becomes related to and connected with the 'illa of the judgments of the same category (jins al-ahkām) and of the same category of objects (jinsīya). Finally, the hukm under consideration for which the ta'līl is sought is of the same category as the hukm which it intends to transcend.[69]

With these conditions specified, Taftāzānī proceeds to examine the takhsīs al-'illa (particularization or restriction of an 'illa) as employed in the doctrine of istihsān. According to Taftāzānī, the 'illa used in the doctrine of istihsān on the basis of its being strong (qawī) cannot be considered as if it is restricted or particularized; and thus, according to Taftāzānī, it violates the asl (Origin). Taftāzānī further maintains that the 'illa used in the istihsān does not hold fast to the actual wordings (alfāz), but is solely based on the figurative application (majāz). The 'illa or adilla (evidences or proofs) used in the hukm (judgment) should be solely conditioned and restricted to the actual wordings rather than its figurative application. Thus, Taftāzānī considers that the qiyās in the form of istihsān is construed in the absence of an 'illa and not on anything which prevents the existing 'illa itself to continue to be used in the qiyās. Further, the 'illa used in the qiyās is considered by the ijmā' (general consensus) as being already established on the basis of evidence and that in itself makes the takhsīs al-'illa (the particularization or restriction of 'illa) as used in the istihsān null and void. Moreover, the original condition of the valid qiyās was not such that there exists any other different 'illa than the one which the qiyās has already employed. Hence, the claim of the upholders of istihsān is not justifiable.[70] Taftāzānī strictly adheres to the notion of jinsīya (sameness of things), such as, iron for iron and equivalent in weight and not to be applied to any other (kind of) things, such as gold in that measure of weight and argues that the 'illa in the asl (Origin) does not include weight. If done so, it would be simply zann (speculation) and not qat'ī (certain).[71] In this connection, Taftāzānī brings out that Sarakhsī allows 'illa not only in cases of jins (genus of things), but also in nau' (species of things) and, thereby, not observing the exact wasf (characteristic or quality) in terms of the jins al-ahkām (sameness of judgments) and jinsīya (sameness of things). Taftāzānī elaborates on this point criticizing that Sarakhsī considers "giving more darhams in addition to what is required to be paid as 'ushr (one-tenth) tax when one passes the territory of Islam" as if it is the same and equivalent to the case when the Prophet used to sell the pants (by weight) and used to give more out of goodness of his heart in addition to what the pants bought (in weight) required.[72] As Taftāzānī says, this case has nothing to do with paying more money in addition to what is required in the payment of 'ushr (one-tenth) taxes. Such a kind of 'illa, if used in the ḥukm (judgment), obviously fails to connect with the aṣl (Origin).[73] It needs to be clarified that Taftāzānī's view in this respect is valid, however, he has misrepresented Sarakhsī's position in this case, as we have already shown in Chapter Five where Sarakhsī discusses the case of a donation (ṣadaqa). If something is given as a donation (ṣadaqa), it is to be considered in terms of the waṣf (characteristic or quality) as an 'illa to be connected with the aṣl (Origin) regarding that jins al-aḥkām (sameness of judgments) and such a donation is not considered as the alms tax (zakāt), since it does not carry the waṣf (characteristic or quality) of intention of the ḥukm (judgment) regarding the zakāt (alms tax). It is simply regarded as a donation, since it lacks the condition in the given donation as being intended for the purpose of alms tax.[74] Furthermore, Taftāzānī employs the argument forwarded by Baṣrī against the 'illa of the doctrine of istiḥsān as being extraneous and quotes him verbatim.[75] Baṣrī leaves unexplained how it is extraneous, but Taftāzānī tries to show it and insists that one should be cautious against what is not inclusive (in the qiyās) for its adoption in a particular case rather than what is accepted in general. This is simply desire (hawā) and inclination (mail) rather than genuine 'illa; and thus, to give preference (tarjīḥ) to one ground (wujh) over all other grounds (wujūh) of what is binding (iḥtijāj) is considered as something extra added by ẓann (speculation).[76] It is arbitrary, as in this way one can also argue in favor of the qiyās by saying that the 'illa of istiḥsān is weaker and that of qiyās is stronger. Only the 'illa connected with the aṣl (Origin) is valid; it can be understood by the reason ('aql), but the reason ('aql) or speculation (ẓann) itself cannot establish the judgment (ḥukm) on the basis of 'illa founded on its own without being connected with the aṣl (Origin).[77]

Finally, Taftāzānī comes to discuss the cases of maqāṣid al-dunyā (purposes of the world) and maqīṣid al-dīn (purposes of the religion) or what roughly corresponds to Sarkhasī's aḥkām al-dunyā, (wordly affairs) and aḥkām al-dīn (religious affairs) and holds that a sharp demarcation and division between the two is not maintainable. Therefore, it cannot be argued that for the maqāṣid al-dunyā (purposes of the world) the 'illa of istiḥsān is valid or justifiable concerning the mu'āmalāt (mutual relations).[78] It should be noted that Taftāzānī's use of the term mu'āmalāt (mutual relations) is in a narrower sense referring to the mu'āmalāt (mutual relations) among the Muslims in normal life and not in the wider sense which includes the mu'āmalāt (mutual relations) of Muslims with other nations concerning the aḥkām al-dunyā (worldly affairs). In light of the foregoing discussions in Chapters Three, Four and Five, it is needless to say that Sarakhsī is able to demonstrate that such subject matters can be brought under and within the framework of sharī'a law.

Taftāzānī concludes his discussion by asserting that the ijtihād (derivation of an independent judgment in the legal matters based on the four sources of Islamic jurisprudence) should be allowed when 'illa is found connected with the aḥkām al-sharī'a (sharī'a laws) and is based on the sharī'a sources, namely the Qur'ān, Ḥadīth, ijmā' and qiyās and which are qaṭ'ī (certain); otherwise, any 'illa not connected with the aḥkām al-sharī'a (sharī'a laws) is to be considered as a product of ẓann (speculation) and not a providence of ijtihād (derivation of an independent judgment in the legal matters based on the four sources of Islamic jurisprudence).[79]

However, Sarakhsī, as shown in the present investigation, has already dealt with such criticisms by establishing that the doctrine has its own validity and, if it is not necessary, he does not replace the 'illa of the doctrine of qiyās. Sarakhsī in his **Uṣūl** and **Mabsūṭ** seeks the 'illa of the doctrine of istiḥsān in the aṣl (Origin) and thereby justifies it in his **Bāb al-Muwāda'a** on the ground that the treaties (muwāda'a) and the mutual relations (mu'āmalāt) of Muslims with other nations fall in a different domain than the usual aḥkām al-dunyā (worldly affairs). Hence, the 'illa to be employed in such cases as these is of a different nature, but nonetheless, it is to be construed within the framework of sharī'a law.

Muḥammad Sa'īd Ramḍān al-Būṭī is one of the few recent jurists who seems to be aware of the real issue regarding the 'illa which is employed in the methodological reasoning (ra'y) of the doctrine of istiṣlāḥ and the doctrine of istiḥsān. Būṭī's **Ḍawābiṭ al-Maṣlaḥa fī al-Sharī'a al-Islāmīya** deals mainly with the maṣlḥā and also with the istiḥsān to a certain extent. It would be impossible to go into all the details regarding Būṭī's discussion of the maṣlaḥa and the maṣlaḥa al-mursala, but on the whole he considers them to be valid so far as the sharī'a is concerned. It is important to observe that he rejects Ṭūfī's position.[80] His criticisms are strictly speaking within the narrow framework of aḥkām al-dīn (religious affairs). Būṭī does not even deal with Riḍā who afterwards tries to develop further Ṭūfī's views. He appears to be unaware of Ṭūfī's and Riḍā's concerns as we shall discuss later. But, nonetheless, Būṭī is the only one who directly goes to Sarakhsī's main point and raises objections against the concept of ease and comfort which Sarakhsī develops in his **Mabsūṭ** and establishes its justification from the Qur'ān and Ḥadīth as already discussed in Chapter Three.

Būṭī's first objection is that the 'illa on the basis of which the doctrine of istiḥsān is considered as its justification cannot be accepted by the general consensus (ijmā'). Sarakhsī has already shown in his **Uṣūl** that any refutation against the 'illa on the ground of general consensus (ijmā') is irrelevant, because the general consensus is in itself not absolute (muṭlaq) and certain (qaṭ'ī), as it changes from time to time and circumstance to circumstance.[81]

Būṭī's second objection is that the 'urf (custom) maṣlaḥa (what is beneficial or expedient) or ḍarūra (necessity) are not recognized as the evidence (dalīl) for comfort or ease, and thus, it is absolutely not allowed to employ them as an 'illa for the abandonment of qiyās in favor of istiḥsān. Būṭī maintains that the istiḥsān lacks necessary 'illa for its employment when it is found contrary to what is established by the qiyās.[82] But, as to why and how it lacks that necessary 'illa, Būṭī even does not consider it important to discuss.

It is interesting to examine one of the several instances that Būṭī describes as a typical view presented by the upholders of the doctrine of juristic preference. The case under consideration is the example given by Būṭī that if a person declares his property is donation (ṣadaqa), then according to the qiyās (doctrine of systematic reasoning), the donation includes all the properties in his possession, but according to the istiḥsān (doctine of juristic preference) it can be restricted to what is incumbent on his property as the alms tax (zakāt).[83] However, such is not the case with Sarakhsī from what we find in his **Bāb al-Muwāda'a**. Here, Sarakhsī maintains that if anyone declares "my property is alms (ṣadaqa)" in the cause of God, it is to be taken by literal interpretation, according to the doctrine of istiḥsān (juristic preference). It is not executed as the alms tax (zakāt).[84] In his **Uṣūl,** Sarakhsī clearly states that if one gives a donation (ṣadaqa) to the poor, it is not considered as the alms tax (zakāt).[85] As a matter of fact, Sarakhsī elaborates on this same point in conjuction and juxtaposition with the validity of the 'illa as employed by the doctrine of istiḥsān (juristic preference) in the form of tarjīḥ (preference) as we have already discussed in Chapter Four. From this it becomes clear that Būṭī is yet not able to perceive the broader perspective from which Sarakhsī pursues his investigation. Sarakhsī's concern is not only the aḥkām al-dīn (religious affairs), wherein he finds the qiyās (doctrine of systematic reasoning) quite adequate, but also the matters of muwāda'a (treaties) and mu'āmalāt (mutual relations) concerning the aḥkām al-dunyā (worldly affairs).

Būṭī's ambiguity becomes more obvious when he concludes his views on the doctrine of istiḥsān (juristic preference). According to Būṭī, the argument offered by the upholders of the doctrine of juristic preference from among the Ḥanafī jurists, is no doubt, valid in the matters concerning the mu'āmalāt (mutual relations), nijāsāt (uncleanliness), furū' (branches of law) and the cases of istithnā' (exception). However from this, according to Būṭī, it cannot be concluded that the doctrine of istiḥsān (juristic preference) as a juristic methodology of reasoning can be considered as being valid.[86]

In short, Būṭī's criticism and his ambivalence toward the validity of the doctrine of juristic preference and especially against Sarakhsī's position shows that Būṭī is not yet quite methodological in his approach and fails to see the main contention and its implications of Sarakhsī's doctrine of juristic preference in juxtaposition with the subject matter of muwāda'a (treaties) and mu'āmalāt (mutual relations).

THE MĀLIKĪ SCHOOL OF THOUGHT:

'Izz al-Dīn ibn 'Abd al-Salām Sulmī (660 A.H./1263 A.D.) employs maṣlaḥa in the tradition of Sufism and entirely in a different context. 'Abd al-Salām's discussion on the doctrine of istiṣlāḥ does not properly address the controversial aspect of the maṣlaḥa regarding its validity in Islamic jurisprudence.

To 'Abd al-Salām, maṣlaḥa means the ladhādha (pleasure) and faraḥ (happiness) and the means leading to them.[87] He divides the maṣāliḥ into two categories: the maṣāliḥ of the hereafter (ākhira) and the maṣāliḥ of this world (dunyā). It is sufficient for our purpose to mention without going into his detailed discussions of maṣlaḥa as the rights (ḥuqūq)[88] that 'Abd al-Salām discusses it within the framework of aḥkām al-dīn (religious affairs). According to 'Abd al-Salām, the maṣlaḥa al-dīn can be based only on the ground of adilla (evidences) from the Qur'ān, Sunna, ijmā' and mu'atabar (acknowledged) qiyās.[89] This kind of maṣlaḥa is used on a lower level and is designed for the aḥkām al-dīn (religious affairs), but on the higher level and keeping in line with the Ṣūfī traditions, 'Abd al-Salām maintains that the maṣlaḥa based on the knowledge (wilāyat) of adhkiyā' and awliyā' (mystic saints) is used for the aḥkām al-ākhira (hereafter affairs).[90] So far as the maṣaliḥ al-dunyā are concerned, they can be known by reason,[91] but in the same vein, 'Abd al-Salām is of the view that since the maṣāliḥ al-dunyā are based on necessity (ḥāja), practice (tajruba), customs ('ādāt) and reasoning (ẓunūn), they are not to be used for the derivation of ḥukm (judgment), since such a ḥukm (judgment) is not based on what God has ordained and, therefore, it is not to be employed for legislating any maṣlaḥa.[92] 'Abd al-Salām also does away with the distinction between the ẓāhir (apparent) and bāṭin (concealed) 'illa. The reasoning (ẓann) is invalid if the ẓāhir (apparent) contradicts the bāṭin (concealed).[93] Thus, to conclude, neither the 'illa of qiyās nor the 'illa of istiḥsān based on what 'Abd al-Salām calls the ẓann (speculation) is properly valid for legislating any sharī'a law in Islamic jurisprudence.

Shihāb al-Dīn al-Qarāfī (684 A.H./1285 A.D.) essentially reinforces Rāzī's position, but at the same time he also directs his attention to the issue regarding the validity of maṣlaḥa, maṣlaḥa al-mursala and istiḥsān. Reinforcing Rāzī's position, on the one hand, he takes objection against the Mu'tazilites that the aṣl (Origin) can be known by the 'aql (human reason) and, on the other, he tries to establish that the maṣlaḥa as such cannot become the basis of legal reasoning, as he maintains that the ijtihād (derivation of an independent judgment in legal matters on the basis of the four sources of Islamic jurisprudence) should be based on textual evidence which cannot be known by the 'aql (human reason).[94] Thus, the ta'līl (inference or the determination of cause of command by logical deduction) can be considered qaṭ'ī (certain), when it is based on the aṣl (Origin) which is absolute (muṭlaq), but the maṣlaḥa as such cannot become the basis of legal reasoning, as it cannot itself become ibāḥa (what is permissible). The reason for not accepting the maṣlaḥa, as Masud also points out, is that it cannot provide absoluteness as required in the sharī'ā law.[95] This becomes clear when one examines what Qarāfī says regarding the maṣlaḥa, maṣlaḥa al-mursala and tarjīḥ (preference).

According to Qarāfī, the maṣlaḥa should be restricted to what is acknowledged by the sharī'a as the ibāḥa (what is permissible). However, it can be extended in the cases of ḥukm (judgment) regarding the prohibitions, such as, the growing of grapes is permissible, but if it is for the purpose of making wine, it is prohibited, and what is neither acknowledged by the sharī'a nor is declared as the ilghā' (null and void) is considered as the maṣlaḥa al-mursala. It is recognized by Mālik. But, when Ghazālī holds that the ḥāja or tatamma (necessity) can be validly employed as the maṣlaḥa, it is not recognized by us (Mālikīs).[96] Qarāfī also insists that one should refrain from the majāz (figurative interpretation of textual wordings) in the use of 'illa.[97] Furthermore, according to Qarāfī, the munāsaba (suitability or affinity) should be entailed in the obtainment of maṣlaḥa which are muṭlaq (absolute); otherwise it is considered as the shubha ṣūrī (equivocal opinion) and not according to the sharī'a law.[98]

Concerning the tarjīḥ (preference) in the case of two amā'ir (indications) with regard to their permissibilities, the choice between the two comes out, as Qarāfī maintains, due to their equality and not because of the permissibility as such and the possibility of establishing the two amā'ir (indications) for an act should only be done by considering one wujh al-iḥtijāj (ground of what is binding) and, thus, the dalīl (evidence) resulting by considering more than one wujūh al-iḥtijāj (grounds of what is binding) cannot be the same.[99] So far as the istiḥsān is concerned, Qarāfī from the very beginning confines qiyās to the qiyās al-jalīy (qiyās based on apparent or explicit 'illa),[100] and thus declares that the istiḥsān is not based on the proper dalīl (evidence) and quotes Baṣrī verbatim arguing that in the qiyās it is not inclusive as a condition that the 'illa be qawī (strong). This is something added by ẓann (speculation) and exercised by the doctrine of istiḥsān in the name of qiyās.[101]

Thus, there are no maṣlaḥa known by 'aql (human reason) or exercise of istiḥsān by an 'illa without the accompaniment of aṣl (Origin) as such. This point of view is reinforced by Qarāfī in support of Rāzī's position and against the Mu'tazilites who hold that God takes consideration of the maṣāliḥ (pl. of maṣlaḥ, what is beneficial or expedient) against the mafāsid (pl. of mafāsada, what is harmful), but there are many mubāḥāt (what is permissible) in which such a consideration is lacking and the Mu'tazilites have never been able to demonstrate that such is not the case.[102]

Recent studies on Abū Isḥāq al-Shāṭibī (790 A.H./1388 A.D.) have shown various aspects of his thoughts. It is true that Shāṭibī to a certain degree is thoroughly permeated with Ghazālī's ideas and thoughts,[103] but from this one should not draw the conclusion, as Masud observes,[104] that he also rejects the maṣlaḥa and, thus, rejects the adaptability of Islamic legal theory to social changes. It is also true, as shown by Riḍā, that Shāṭibī believes and strives to show the immutability of Islamic law. As Masud has shown in his study, there is no doubt that Shāṭibī's thought addresses the issue of social change and deals with the aḥkām al-dunyā (or what Shāṭibī calls the 'ādāt or customs on the sharī'a level) where changes are not only possible but are necessary, although ultimately on the level of awākhir (hereafters), such a distinction does not hold.

This emerges from the general position which Shāṭibī holds. According to Shāṭibī, there are two kinds of obligations: the obligations under the category of 'ibādāt (religious observances) which are absolute (muṭlaq) and not subject to change; and the obligations under the category of 'ādāt (customs), including the mu'āmalāt (mutual relations), which are relative and subject to change. This distinction is maintained on the first level which is that of shar'ī (pertaining to the sharī'a laws), though both may become ta'abbud (obedience) on the second level which is that of the mukallaf (subject to legal obligation).

Shāṭibī establishes this general position by focusing on the maṣlaḥa and directing his attack on the bid'a (innovation) in his works **al-Muwāfqāt** and **al-I'tiṣām**. Shāṭibī identifies the maqāṣid al-sharī'a (objectives of the sharī'a) with the maṣlaḥa in **al-Muwāfqāt**; and his discussions in **al-I'tiṣām** regarding the maṣlaḥa al-mursala (maṣlaḥa not supported by the Text) and the istiḥsān are in relation to the bid'a, all of which are not allowed so far as the uṣūl al-dīn (religious principles) are concerned. But nonetheless, the maṣlaḥa or the istiḥsān, as we shall see later, are neither totally relative and arbitrary principles nor strictly tied to the qiyās or specific legal Texts of sharī'a. The maṣlaḥa is connected to social needs at one end, and at the other end inductively supported by the sharī'a. It is, thus, "not a special form of analogy (qiyās), nor is it an extra legal method of expediency to provide an area of flexibility in legal reasoning along with more strict elements of the laws."[105] To Shāṭibī, the maṣlaḥa is an integral principle that unifies the sharī'a, provides stability, and gives direction to legal changes.

Thus, Shāṭibī stresses that no innovation can be accepted in the 'ibādāt (religious observances), whereas in the 'ādāt (customs) changes are possible. The matters related to the 'ibādāt belong to the maṣāliḥ which are known only to God. They cannot be explained by reason, and, hence, cannot be extended by the qiyās (analogy) to other situations, whereas the case is different concerning the matters of 'ādāt (customs). Not only are they based on the maṣlaḥa, but, the commands in the sharī'a relating to the 'ādāt usually provide reason, indicating that these maṣāliḥ can be grasped by human reason and are extendable by the analogy (qiyās).[106]

As mentioned, Shāṭibī's general position emerges by his identifying the maṣāliḥ with the maqāṣid. Therefore, we shall first clarify and summarize his views on the maṣlaḥa from **al-Muwāfqāt** and supplement them with the views from **al-I'tiṣām** on the ẓann (speculation), bid'a (innovation) and their relation to themaṣlaḥa al-mursala and the istiḥsān.

Shāṭibī defines the maṣlaḥa as "that which concerns the subsistence of human life, the completion of man's livelihood and acquisition of what the emotional and intellectual qualities require of him, in an absolute sense."[107] The maṣāliḥ belong either to this world or to the world hereafter. Now, Shāṭibī divides the maṣaliḥ into ḍarūrī (necessary), ḥājī (needed) and taḥsīnī (commendable). The ḍarūrī (necessary) consists of dīn (religion), nafs (life), nasl (descendants), māl (property) and 'aql (reason), as Ghazālī had specified. The ḥājiyāt (pl. of ḥājī, what is needed) expands (tawassu') or promotes the maqāṣid (objectives) to remove the impediments or obstacles in the way of maqāṣid (objectives), such as the fasting, etc.; in the area of 'ādāt (customs), such as the lawfulness of hunting, and in the mu'āmalāt (mutual relations), such as the permission for qirāḍ (money lending). The taḥsīniyāt cover what conforms to the customs of the people, and the cases of 'ibādāt (religious observances), such as cleanliness, the 'ādāt (customs), such as good manners and the mu'āmlāt (mutual relations), such as selling of unclean articles.[108]

The above classification of the maṣlaḥa into various categories shows that the maṣlaḥa, according to Shāṭibi, covers both the 'ibādāt (religious observances) or what Sarakhsī calls the aḥkām al-dīn (religious affairs) and the 'ādāt (customs) which include the mu'āmlāt (mutual relations) or what Sarakhsī calls the aḥkām al-dunyā, with the important difference that the maṣlaḥa pertaining to the former are muṭlaq (absolute), kullī (universal and not relative and subjective, namely, ẓannī), whereas the maṣlaḥa pertaining to the latter are not. That is because the maṣlaḥa covering the 'ādāt (customs) and mu'āmalāt (mutual relations) can be the results of the ahwā' al-nafs (personal likings), manāfī (personal advantage) nayl al-shahawāt (fulfillment of passionate desires) and aghrāḍ (personal interests) and, thus, not a consideration of sharī'a. This is because in the 'ibādāt (religious observances), the consideration of maṣlaḥa is the ākhira (hereafter) and in the 'ādāt (customs), it is dunyā (this world).[109]

Keeping this in view, now we proceed to analyze what Shaṭibī discusses in the section, "The difference between the bid'a (innovation), the maṣlaḥa al-mursala (the maṣlaḥa not supported by the Text) and the istishsān" in his **al-I'tiṣām.**[110] In order to systematize his views on the maṣlaḥa al-mursala and the istiḥsān andcome to an exact conclusion regarding their validity for the employment in the uṣūl al-dīn (principles of religion), we first need to examine his view on the bid'a (innovation) and the ẓann (speculation) and their relation to the maṣlaḥa and the istiḥsān; and, second, we need to analyze to what extent and in what ways, according to Shāṭibī, the maṣlaḥa al-mursala and the istiḥsān can be said to be in valid for their use in the sharī'a law.

Shāṭibī holds the view in general that whatever is unprecedented in the sharī'a by textual evidence is bid'a (innovation), whether it can be from the Ṣūfī doctrines and practices or it can be from the fuqahā' (jurists), such as the doctrine of maṣlaḥa al-mursala in the Mālikī school of thought, or the doctrine of istiḥsān in the Ḥanafī school of thought. This is not to say that Shāṭibī rejects them altogether if they are harmless; what he is after is that so far as the uṣūl al-dīn and 'ibādāt are concerned, they do not go further. The main targets of his entire criticism are the innovations of the Ṣūfī doctrines and practices and his criticism on the maṣlaḥa al-mursala and the istiḥsān is that those who exercise these doctrines maintain that they are extra sources for determining the sharī'a law[111] and, therefore, they are claiming the validity of these doctrines on their own accord. This is according to Shāṭibī quite inappropriate and ghulū' (exceeding of the proper bounds of sharī'a.)[112] As a matter of fact, when one examines closely the sections on the maṣlaḥa al-mursala and the istiḥsān, then the contention of what Shāṭibī claims becomes clear. Here Shāṭibī maintains that tarakhkhuṣ (legal concession), istithnā' (exception)[113] and murā'āt al-khilāf (allowance for disagreement in opinion)[114] used in the maṣlaḥa al-mursala or the 'illa used in the doctrine of istiḥsān, are considered as the maṣlaḥa which are appropriate or valid, but only in the area of 'ādāt (customs) and nothing further.

This becomes more clear when one analyzes what Shaṭibī asserts about the ẓann (speculation), as it is the reason for rejecting bid'a (innovation). According to Shāṭibī, first, the ẓann is contrary to the aṣl (Origin) and is simply an opinion of the one who holds it without dalīl (evidence) and thus without any validity, but if it concerns the furū' (branches of law) and is based on dalīl (evidence), it is valid in the sharī'a law.[115] Thus, the ẓann is objectionable except in the furū' and when it is accompanied by dalīl (evidence). Second, the ẓann which prefers one thing over its opposite without evidence is objectionable for its arbitrariness, and that is, following the likings of the one who exercises such a ẓann, but if the ẓann is related with the dalīl (evidence), it is not objectionable on the whole and is excluded from what is called following one's liking.[116] Third, there are two aspects of ẓann, one which is based on the aṣl (Origin) which is qaṭ'ī (certain) and that kind of ẓann is valid; and the other, when the ẓann is based on the aṣl (Origin) which is not qaṭ'ī, but is based on something not in accordance with the aṣl (Origin), then it is objectionable. The use of ẓann is operative only in the realm of 'ādāt (customs), which includes the mu'āmalāt (mutual relations).[117] With this background, we can now focus on the doctrine of istiḥsān and the maṣlaḥa al-mursala in relation to what Shāṭibī has said of the ẓann and its permissibility.

In his discussion on the istiḥsān and maṣlaḥ al-mursala, Shaṭibī asserts that what is claimed to be exercised in the name of istiḥsān, whether on the basis of 'aql (reason) or sharī'a, is but what the one who exercises holds it to be the istiḥsān. So far as the sharī'a is concerned, it is finished and done with and there is no need to add anything further on the Qur'ān, Sunna, ijmā' or what is instituted by the qiyās and istidlāl (evidence).[118] Thus, there is no use in calling it the istiḥsān, for it refers in its use to the evidence which is already provided and if it does not, then it is a bid'a.[119] So is the case with maṣlaḥa al-mursala, when it is used as ḍarūrī (necessary), it simply belongs to the mu'āmalāt (mutual relations) and is used to facilitate what the maṣlaḥa itself intends to promote, namely, the maqāṣid al-sharī'a belonging to the ta'bbud (obedience). As such the maṣlaḥa al-mursala does not carry any weight so far as the sharī'a is concerned. It is also not different in the case of murā'āt al-khilāf (allowance for the disagreement of opinion). It is essentially the ta'ārūd al-adilla (contradiction found in evidences) and, therefore, considered as a problem posited false.[120] Thus, Shāṭibī's main object is to bring out the immutability of sharī'a law while simultaneously dealing with the aḥkām al-dīn (religious affairs) or, what he terms as the 'ibādāt (religious observances) and aḥkām al-dunyā (worldly affairs) or, what he terms as the 'ādāt (customs) which includes the mu'āmalāt (mutual relations) and establishes that no inovation (bid'a) is introduced and permitted in the 'ibādāt (religious observances). But, so far as the aḥkām al-dunyā (worldly affairs) are concerned, the maṣlaḥa al-mursala and istiḥsān become necessary in order to adapt to change. Furthermore, so far as the furū' (branches of law) are concerned, the employment of ẓann, as Shāṭibī coins it, is perfectly valid.

Thus, it can be said that Shāṭibī's position regarding the istiḥsān as a methodological reasoning in Islamic jurisprudence does not run against Sarakhsī's position, as Shāṭibī recognizes its validity within the aḥkām al-dunyā (worldly affairs) and Sarakhsī's treatment of muwāda'a (treaties) and mu'āmalāt (mutual relations) concerning the aḥkām al-dunyā (worldly affairs) deals essentially with that aspect. But, Sarakhsī tries to establish it as an autonomous discipline with the application of and in juxtaposition with the doctrine of istiḥsān seeking its justification in the aṣl (Origin) and from the sharī'a law and certainly not exceeding their bounds. As a matter of fact, Shāṭibī tries to establish to a certain extent and show how the maqāṣid al-sharī'a (objectives of sharī'a) provide unity to the 'ādāt (customs), as Sarakhsī strives to unify the muwāda'a (treaties) and mu'āmalāt (mutual relations) within the framework of sharī'ā law. But, to conclude, Shāṭibī does not treat the subject matter concerning the aḥkām al-dunyā (worldly affairs) in any systematic way by any method of juristic reasoning (ra'y) on a doctrinal basis and subject them to any analysis and systematization so that they are incorporated and encompassed within the framework of sharī'a laws as does Sarakhsī.

THE ḤAMBALĪ SCHOOL OF THOUGHT:

Abū Muḥammad 'Alī bin Aḥmad bin Sa'īd ibn Ḥazm (456 A.H./1064 A.D.) was at first an ardent follower of the Shafi'ī school of thought, but later on he went over to the opinions of the Ẓāhirīya school of thought of which he became a devoted advocate. As it has already been mentioned, the conclusions which follow from the position held by the Ḥambalī and Ẓāhirīya schools of thought against the use of ra'y (juristic reasoning) are essentially not different, therefore, the jurists from both of these schools are treated under the Ḥambalī school of thought.

Ibn Ḥazm's position is that the details of legal deduction or inference not resting on the Text and traditions (aḥādīth) must be rejected. He discusses the istiḥsān in his **Iḥkām fī Uṣūl al-Aḥkām** by attacking its advocates who justify its use on the basis of the Qur'ānic verse, "those who listen to a testimony and follow the best of it are those whom God guides, and are most understanding."[121] According to Ibn Ḥazm, this verse is an evidence against rather than in support of the doctrine of istiḥsān because the verse does not say that they should follow what they consider best (ma istaḥsanū), but what is best (aḥsana).[122] Moreover, it is impossible that all jurists would like the same thing, considering the difference in their inclinations. It follows that the istiḥsān is a passion (shahwā), the following of one's inclination and an error (ḍalāl).[123] Furthermore, we may ask the upholders of the doctrine of istiḥsān: "what is the difference between what you like and what someone does not like and vice versa, and, which one of the two is more deserving of truth."[124] From this, it becomes evident that ibn Ḥazm leaves completely unexamined the justification of istiḥsān which the advocates of the doctrine, such as Sarakhsī, strive to establish by showing that the 'illa employed in the doctine is validly based on and connected with the aṣl (Origin). Thus, ibn Ḥazm rejects istiḥsān in its outer form without taking into consideration and examining juristically the real issue regarding the 'illa employed in the doctrine of istiḥsān.

In the Ḥambalī school of thought, Najum al-Din al-Ṭūfī (716 A.H./1316 A.D.) and in recent times Rashīd Riḍā (1243 A.H./1865 A.D.) address the issue of maṣlaḥa in the methodological reasoning (ra'y) and focus once again on the maṣlaḥa as well as istiḥsān which can become the basis for siyāsa (administrative organizations and policies) to adapt to and meet with the changes and dynamism of the modern world.

Ṭūfī holds the position for the precedence of maṣlaḥa over the Text and Sunna.[125] He also holds that the istiḥsān is valid, as it becomes clear from his statement that "istiḥsān means ruling in which a benefit to the community (umma) is confirmed.

It is really not a 'hidden qiyās' as sometimes alleged; the latter explanation was invented to escape the Ḥadīth partisan's allegations that istiḥsān raised personal opinion to the status of an independent source of law."[126] Ṭūfī's position is basedon the Ḥadīth, "no injury and no counter injury"[127] and claims that all specific rules enunciated in the Text and Sunna should be subordinated to it.[128] According to Ṭūfī, this calls for the admission of consideration for maṣlaḥa in all cases of law except those which are, strictly speaking, religious laws ('ibādāt).[129]

Ṭūfī's position for the precedence of maṣlaḥa over the Text and Sunna is mainly based on the arguments that it has more universal backing; it brings about the agreement among the four Sunnite schools of thought which is demanded by Law, and also that there are examples found in the Sunna, which contradicted consideration of maṣlaḥa and yet the latter was preferred.[130] However, as Kerr observes, Ṭūfī's position is controversial, as it is based on a weak Ḥadīth, and also, as pointed out by Masud, it fails to elaborate on a concrete criteria of maṣāliḥ regarding how it is decided especially in a case where it is a question of choosing among more than one maṣlaḥa.[131]

Riḍā leans heavily on Ṭūfī's position, but goes further from it and considers that the true distinction between the religious and non-religious is not what is traditionally maintained as between the 'ibādāt (religious) and mu'āmalāt (mutual relations), but between the 'ibādāt (religious observances) plus those parts of the mu'āmalāt (mutual relations) that have religious or moral significance and other parts of mu'āmalāt which are of administrative organizations or practical convenience. The fixed principles of legal cases of mu'āmalāt (mutual relations) are only of a general character, allowing considerable adaptation by successive generations of Muslims in light of the demands of their worldly welfare, while it is only the 'ibādāt (religious observances) that do not admit to interpretive change.[132]

From this, it becomes evident that with Riḍā, the use of maṣlaḥa is meant to reform in practice the structure of the political and social institutions and bring dynamism to those institutions in order to accommodate the changes demanded for the welfare and needs of the Muslim communities in the modern world, but it fails to provide any theoretical basis within the framework of sharī'a law by a definite doctrinal approach to subject and incorporate such material facts which arise due to the dynamism of the modern world and enter into consideration in the realm of mu'āmalāt (mutual relations) of Muslims with other nations of the world, as we find with Sarakhsī.

Thus, while Riḍā makes the case of maṣlaḥa as a general principle for the structure of administrative organizations and policies, Sarakhsī demonstrates how such material facts regarding the subject matters of the muwāda'a (treaties) and mu'āmalāt (mutual relations) can be subjected in juxtaposition by the doctrine of istiḥsān within the framework of sharī'a law.

It becomes clear from this overview that in the course of the historical development of Islamic jurisprudence, the employment of ra'y as a method of juristic reasoning in the form of the doctrine of istiṣlāḥ and the doctrine of istiḥsān becomes developed, focused and exactly defined in terms of waṣf (characteristic or quality) as the maṣlaḥa (what is beneficial or expedient) that entails munāsaba (suitability or affinity) and is restricted (takhṣīṣ) by the formal qualifications of the sameness of judgments (jins al-aḥkām) and the sameness of things (jinsīya) for the derivation of an independent judgment (ḥukm) in the Mālikī doctrine of istiṣlāḥ, and, correspondingly, what amounts to be its equivalent in the Ḥanafī school of thought is that the 'illa employed in the doctrine of istiḥsān is to be based on and connected with the aṣl (Origin).

To conclude, the controversy regarding the use of ra'y (juristic reasoning) centered around this aspect of the doctrine of istiḥsān and the doctrine of istiṣlāḥ in the historical development of Islamic jurisprudence. The objections which were raised by the jurists from the Mālikī and Shāfi'ī schools of thought came to surface against the validity of the doctrine of istiḥsān employed by the jurists from the Ḥanafī school of thought. This was mainly due to the fact that istiḥsān was kept unsystematized and undefined. Sarakhsī defines the doctrine of istiḥsān and systematizes it to its fullest as a juristic methodology by analyzing and including all the aspects of 'illa against the use of which objections surfaced in the course of the historical development of Islamic jurisprudence and justifies its validity by showing that the 'illa used in the doctrine of istiḥsān is based on and connected with the aṣl (Origin). But more importantly, Sarakhsī incorporates the subject matters of muwāda'a (treaties) and mu'āmalāt (mutual relations) concerning the aḥkām al-dunyā (worldly affairs) as an autonomous discipline in juxtaposition with his doctrine of istiḥsān, in contrast to and comparison with what is not provided by other jurists from all four schools of thought in the history of Islamic jurisprudence.

CONCLUSION AND AFTERTHOUGHT

The recognition of the use of ra'y (reasoning) in the historical development of Islamic jurisprudence has played a vital role. As a matter of fact, the use of ra'y (reasoning) was responsible for broadening the scope of Islamic jurisprudence since it was only by the use of ra'y (reasoning), the Muslim jurists in the Antiquity were able to incorporate and absorb into Islamic jurisprudence the new material facts which arose with the expansion of Islam and resulted in their mu'āmalāt (mutual relations) concerning the aḥkām al-dunyā (worldly affairs) with other nations. Howevermuch the use of ra'y (reasoning) was recognized in practice, it did not go unchallenged on the theoretical and juristic level. The questions arose as to its limitations and the extent to which its use is justifiable by the sharī'a law and, thus, it became controversial. It may even seem to an outside observer standing aloof from and apart at a distance of more than a thousand years, that the history of Islamic jurisprudence is filled with controversies and ambiguities, engaged in details of no consequence.

However, a closer look from inside, sifting and filtering through this webb of ambiguities due to the difference of opinions by the jurists boils down to the question of the validity of the use of ra'y (reasoning) in its various forms in the history of Islamic jurisprudence in the four (Sunnite) schools of thought. As a historical fact in Islamic jurisprudence, the controversy regarding the use of ra'y (reasoning) centered around its use in the form of the doctrine of istiḥsān (juristic preference) and the doctrine of istiṣlāḥ (consideration of maṣlaḥa, namely, what is beneficial and expedient) and their validity within the framework of sharī'a law. Both of these doctrines were an attempt to find the material principle which can justify the use of ra'y (reasoning), though both differed from each other in the interpretation of it. In the Mālikī school of thought, it was formulated in terms of maṣlaḥa (what is beneficial or expedient) which should observe and meet the criteria of the waṣf (characteristic or quality) as the maṣlaḥa (what is beneficial or expedient) which is munāsib (suitable) to the aṣl (Origin) qualified by the formal condition of carrying the sameness of judgments (jins al-aḥkām) and the sameness of things (jinsīya); and in the Ḥanafī school of thought, it was interpreted in terms of an 'illa used in the doctrine of istiḥsān as being based on and connected with the aṣl (Origin).

On the one hand, in the Mālikī school of thought, the maṣlaḥa (what is beneficial or expedient) gradually became a proper methodological approach and, so to say, became fully developed and defined, but nontheless and prominently it remained confined to the aḥkām al-dīn (religious affairs) and only in dire need to be allowed and accommodated in the aḥkām al-dunyā (worldy affairs). On the other hand in the Ḥanafī school of thought, the doctrine of istiḥsān was somehow left undefined, as one finds in the history of Islamic jurisprudence. As a result, even an outside observer could notice that severe objections were raised against the use and validity of istiḥsān (doctrine of juristic preference) mostly by the jurists from the Mālikī and Shāfi'ī schools of thought. Thus, the istiḥsān became more of a center of controversy and, that is not to say that the istiṣlāḥ came to be accepted in its entirety and by all the jurists from the Mālikī and Shāfi'ī schools of thought. It remained also controversial, but to a certain extent, it drew less attention in the controversy compared to the doctrine of istiḥsān. This can be attributed to the fact, as it becomes obvious from our investigation, that the earlier jurists from the Ḥanafī school of thought before Sarakhsī used the doctrine of istiḥsān (juristic preference) vaguely without defining it properly and, much less, they attempted to examine systematically the validity of the 'illa employed in the doctrine as being found in and connected with the aṣl (Origin).

Sarakhsī is one of the very few jurists from among the Ḥanafī jurists who undertakes to define and systematize the doctrine of istiḥsān (juristic preference) taking into consideration all the criticisms and the objections raised against the validity of the 'illa used in the doctrine of istiḥsān (juristic preference) and seeks its justification, independently of the doctrine of qiyās (systematic reasoning)by analyzing and examining the 'illa used in the doctrine of istiḥsān (juristic preference) on the basis of and as being connected with the aṣl (Origin).

But, of much greater importance and what sets Sarakhsī apart from all the jurists in all the four (Sunnite) schools of thought of Islamic jurisprudence, including the Ḥanafī jurists such as Shaybānī to whom Sarakhsī's works are generally attributed and considered as if Sarakhsī is simply narrating and expounding on Shaybānī's works, is that he not only brings out the doctrine of istiḥsān (juristic preference) to its completion in all its aspects, but also at the same time, subjects the contents of muwāda'a (treaties) and mu'āmalāt (mutual relations) concerning the aḥkām al-dunyā (worldly affairs) in juxtaposition with the doctrine of istiḥsān (juristic preference) in order to broaden and enhance the scope of Islamic jurisprudence by incorporating all the material facts. Furthermore, Sarakhsī demonstrates how such matters can be embodied and embedded as an autonomous discipline within the framework of sharī'a law rather than considering them as falling outside its realm and not within its bounds, such as we find with most of the Ḥanafī, Mālikī, Shāfi'ī and Ḥambalī jurists, some of whom are accutely aware of the fact that the subject matters of muwāda'a (treaties) and mu'āmalāt concerning the (aḥkām al-dunyā) worldly affairs are of crucial importance, but they do not yet bring these subject matters into focus. Sarakhsī, unlike other Muslim jurists, does not give them simply marginal accommodation subsummed under the aḥkām al-dīn (religious affairs) and eased them under the case of dire necessity or such other factors, but Sarakhsī also embodies and adopts them within the framework of sharī'a law and finds their justification on that accord to adapt and adjust with the dynamic changes in the aḥkām al-dunyā (worldy affairs). With Sarakhsī, we find that these subject matters are brought within the framework of sharī'a law as the legitimate and autonomous discipline.

This aspect of Sarakhsī's original thought is not perceived properly. It is thought provoking and certainly improves on the doctrinal use of ra'y (reasoning) in the form of the doctrine of istiḥsān (juristic preference). One would have expected the importance of it not only as a structural basis on the theoretical level, but also in practice, in view of the developments in the systems of law in various Muslim countries, especially when one considers the fact that beginning from the seventeenth century onward and continuing at present, the Islamic system of law and jurisprudence in practice has not been efficiently operative, if one does not say that it has been dormant. In the conflicts, confusions and ambiguities which are the scenario of the present day Muslim world when it comes to deal with the adaptation and adjustments to the dynamic changes occurring in the global interaction and influences of cultural, social and religious values with other nations, Sarakhsī's doctrine of istiḥsān (juristic preference) could have been taken as a reference point and guideline for the further development and refinement of the doctrine in light of new material facts which are occurring in the modern Muslim world.

With this, it is not said that to a certain extent such kinds of attempts have not been made in the Muslim countries. The intellectual movements in the past beginning with Muḥammad 'Abduh (1323 A.H./1905), Jamāl al-Dīn Afghānī (1315 A.H./1897) and others are not unknown to anyone familiar with the modern Islam. They have certainly brought an awakening in the Muslim world on the general level. The name of Rashīd Riḍā (1243 A.H./1865 A.D) and many others in the recent past register in one's mind and their voices echo in one's ears to bring changes in the Muslim world. It is true that in some ways these thinkers have stirred up the emotions in the Muslim world, but they are by no means to be labeled as the systematic thinkers who proceed to change the face of the world of Islam with any methodological approach to deal with the process of assimilitation, adaptation and adjustment to the new material facts arising due to the dynamic and rapid changing situation in the present day modern world.

Sarakhsī provides the framework to structure the material facts to be incorporated in a systematic and gradual way with a viable method of reasoning (ra'y) in the form of the doctrine of istiḥsān (juristic preference) within the framework of Islamic jurisprudence and sharī'a law. This contribution of Sarakhsī needs to be recognized and should be made an integral part of the legacy of Islamic jurisprudence in its historical development.

APPENDIX

Sarakhsī's Life and Works as Documented in Various Sources

A. TRANSLATED FROM THE **KITĀB AL-FAWĀ'ID AL-BAHĪYA FĪ AL-TARĀJIM AL-ḤANAFĪYA** BY 'ABD AL-ḤAIY LAKANAWĪ:[1]

(Muḥammad bin Aḥmad) abī Suhal Abū Bakr Shams al-A'imma al-Sarakhsī was a leading authority and a statesman who as an original thinker discussed and inquired into the principles of (Islamic) jurisprudence. He was credited by Kamāl Pāshā as being one of the greatest scholars of Islamic jurisprudence of his time. He became attached (as a student) to 'Abd al-'Azīz al-Ḥalwānī and took lessons from him until he was certified and became one of the greatest scholars of his time. It is said that he died around 490 A.H./1096 A.D. It is also said that he died around 500 A.H./1106 A.D. With him studied eminent scholars like 'Abd al-'Azīz bin 'Omar Māza, Maḥmūd bin 'Abd al-'Azīz Ūzgandī, Ruknuddīn Mas'ūd bin Ḥasan, and 'Othmān bin 'Alī bin Muḥammad al-Baykandī, who was still studying with Sarakhsī who was in the prison and dictated to him the **Mabsūṭ** which consists of twenty five volumes. Sarakhsī was detained in the pit because of his advice to the ruler. Sarakhsī gave dictation from his memory, without having any reading material at hand, while being confined below in the pit and his companions (students) would take dictation standing above. Sarakhsī said, at the end of the **Sharḥ al-'Ibādāt**, that it is the last **Sharḥ (Commentary)** on the **Kitāb al-'Ibādāt** with clear and concise explanations dictated by the prisoner before the group of people and gathering. Sarakhsī said at the end of **Sharḥ al-Iqrār**, that he concludes the **Sharḥ al-Iqrār** containing the inward meaning (ma'ānī) and is the dictation by the prisoner in the peril of confinement. To him (also) belong the **Uṣūl -al-Fiqh** and the **Sharḥ al-Kabīr**, which he dictated in the prison. When he reached the chapter al-Shurūṭ,[2] he was released from the suffering of confinement and set free. He left for Farghāna in the last part of his life and came to the house of Amīr Ḥasan and fulfilled his wish by completing the dictation. (The compilers say:) Sarakhsī belonged to the place called S-R-KHS,"s" pronounced as "sa", "r" pronounced as "ra" and "kh" is pronounced without a vowel. It is an ancient city of Khorāsān. It is named as Sarakhs after the name of the person who built it. Sam'ānī mentions that Dhūl al-Qarnayn restored it. I have read his **Sharḥ al-Kabīr.** God be praised. We find in it the discussions of juristic matters pertaining to Islamic laws and is very useful as it contains many traditions (aḥādīth). The traditions (aḥādīth) are narrated with the chain of transmissions (riwāya). In the city of learning, he was certified by Shams al-A'imma 'Abd al-'Azīz al-Ḥalwānī and died around (500 A.H./1106 A.D.).[3] He was a great scholar of Islamic jurisprudence, and soon it became known that he dictated his **Mabsūṭ** without referring to any books. To him belong the **Uṣūl al-Fiqh** and **Sharḥ al-Siyar al-Kabīr**, both of which he dictated while he was being confined in the pit due to his advice to the ruler. His students gathered above the pit and wrote down what he dictated.[4] When Sarakhsī reached the chapter al-Shurūṭ, he was released from the confinment and he left for Farghāna where Amīr Ḥasan treated him with hospitality. His students came to him and Sarakhsī finished his dictation. To him is (also) attributed the **Sharḥ al-Ṭaḥāwī**;[5] It is said that Shāfi'ī committed one thousand and three hundred complete quires to memory. According to the **Ṭabaqāt al-Qārī**, Sarakhsī dictated his **Mabsūṭ** consisting of about fifteen volumes while he was confined in the prison at Ūzgand. He was imprisoned because of the advice to the ruler. He was one of our greatest scholars from Transoxiana on Islamic jurisprudence and the furū' (branches of law). He died in 483 A.H./1099 A.D.

B. TRANSLATED FROM THE **AL-JAWĀHIR AL-MUḌĪYA** BY IBN ABŪ AL-WAFĀ AL-QURASHĪ:[6]

(Muḥammad) bin Aḥmad bin Sahal Abū Bakr al-Sarakhsī is repeatedly mentioned in the **Hidāyāt** as the greatest Imām Shams al-A'imma, the author of the **Mabsūṭ** and other works. He was one of the most outstanding among the greatest authorities in Islamic jurisprudence. He was the most eminent scholar who discussed the fundamental laws of Islamic jurisprudence with originality of thought. He was attached (as a student) to the Imām Abū Muḥammad 'Abd al-'Azīz al-Ḥalwānī, until he was certified and became an example of his time. He developed a reputation from his writings, and became distinguished among his peers. It became known that he dictated the **Mabsūṭ**, which consists of about fifteen volumes, while he was confined in the prison at Ūzgand and was destitute of any worldly possessions because he was one of those who followed the firm and clear way and gave his statement of advice to the ruler, so that he could have his lot on the way of judgment. Indeed, God accepts those who are pious and takes care of those who are righteous and does not lead them to the deceit of the rulers or deprives reward to those who deserve it. Sarakhsī said in his **Mabsuṭ**, when he was finished with the **Sharḥ al-'Ibādāt,** that this was the last **Sharḥ (Commentary)** on the **Kitāb al-'Ibādāt** with concise explanations and clearer inward meaning (ma'ānī) dictated by the prisoner before the group of people and gatherings. He said at the end of the **Kitāb al-Ṭalāq** that this is the last **Sharḥ (Commentary)** on the **Kitāb al-Ṭalāq**, which has far reaching impact in deeper meaning (ma'ānī). The prisoner dictated it while being confined and afflicted with the peril of loneliness, praying for the Prophet, who made his ascension to the seven heavens, and for his companions who were pious and giving. His prayers may multiply and last till the day of appropriation. The slave of God wrote it behind the closed doors. He said at the end of the **Kitāb al-I'tāq** that he concludes the **Sharḥ (Commentary)** on the **Kitāb al-I'tāq** dealing with the cases of agreement and disagreements of opinions among various jurists. He embraced gladly the imprisonment which came from above. He said at the end of the **Kitāb al-Iqrār** that he concludes the **Sharḥ (Commentary)** on the **Kitāb al-Iqrār**, containing the secret of sectrets. The prisoner dictated it at the place of wickedness, praying for the select (the Prophet). Abū Bakr Muḥammad bin Ibrāhīm al-Ḥuṣayrī, Abū 'Omar Māza, 'Othmān bin 'Alī bin Muḥammad Baykandī, and Abū Ḥafṣ 'Omar bin Ḥabīb, who was the grandfather from the side of the mother of the author of the **Hidāya**, studied under him (Sarakhsī) and (Abū Ḥafṣ) died around 490 A.H./1096 A.D.

C. TRANSLATED FROM THE **KASHF AL-ẒUNŪN** BY ḤĀJĪ KHALĪFA:[7]

The **Siyar al-Kabīr and Siyar al-Ṣaghīr**:

The works in Islamic jurisprudence were authored by Muḥammad al-Shaybānī, an associate of Abū Ḥanīfa. It is his last work after leaving Irāq and, therefore, Abū Ḥafṣ does not mention it. Shams al-A'imma 'Abd al-'Azīz bin Aḥmad al-Ḥalwānī and Shams al-A'imma Muḥmmad bin Aḥmad al-Sarakhsī wrote commentary on the **al-Siyar al-Kabīr**. Sarakhsī died in the year 483 A.H./1090

A.D. or 486 A.H./1093 A.D., and it is also said that he died around 490 A.H./1096 A.D. He said at the end of his commentary (**Sharḥ**) that the humble servant of God finished the dictation while being in the peril of solitary confinement afflicted by the dangerous sovereign and instigated by the worst possible unbeliever. He began his **Sharḥ** at Ūzgand in the last days of his suffering and came to an end (by the disappearance of cruelty) at Marghīnān in the fifth month of 480 A.H./1087 A.D.[8]

He (Shaybānī) does not narrate from Abū Yūsuf, because of the deep rooted hatred which took place between them. Whenever it was necessary to refer to him, he says, it has been narrated to us by a trustworthy authority. The reason of his writing **al-Siyar al-Kabīr** was that **al-Siyar al-Ṣaghīr** came to the hands of Awzā'ī (157 A.H./774 A.D.) and he asked, "to whom does this book belong?" and he was told, "Muḥammad, the 'Irāqī". He said that the 'Irāqīs do not have such writings, as they do not have any knowledge of the discipline of siyar. It reached the ears of Muḥammad (al-Shaybānī) and he wrote **al-Siyar al-Kabīr**. Awzā'ī took a glance at it and said, "if it had not contained any tradtions (aḥādīth), I would have said that it was written down from his imagination." Thereafter, he ordered copies dispatched to ninety of his offices and hurried on the cart to the door of the Caliph, who was highly surprised and called al-Shaybānī the greatest man of his time and sent his children to attend al-Shaybānī's lectures. Ismā'īl bin Tauba, a man of great learning, was present with them. There exists no more any such a narrator. Jamāluddīn Maḥmūd bin 'Abd al-Sayyad al-Bukhārī al-Ḥuṣayrī al-Ḥanafī, who died in 636 A.H./1238 A.D., wrote a commentary on it.

D. TRANSLATED FROM **TĀJ AL-TARĀJIM FĪ ṬABAQĀT AL-ḤANAFĪYA** BY IBN QUṬLŪBUGHĀ:[9]

Muḥammad bin Aḥmad 'Abū Sahal al-Sarakhsī Shams al-A'imma, the author of the **Mabsūṭ** was certified in Islamic jurisprudence from 'Abd al-'Azīz al-Ḥalwānī. He dictated his **Mabsūṭ** while he was held in the prison. Abū Bakr bin Ibrāhīm al-Ḥuṣayrī and others studied Islamic jurisprudence with him. He died around 500 A.H./1106 A.D. He was a scholar of foremost rank in Islamic jurisprudence.

I was told that he dictated the **Mabsūṭ** from his memory. It is stated in the **Masālik** that he used to have gatherings of great numbers of students. It is said that Shāfi'ī committed three hundred quires to memory. He (the author of **Masālik**) said that Shāfi'ī committed to memory excessively, but it is estimated that Sarakhsī committed thirteen thousand quires to memory. I am told that he did not refer to any books (while dictating) and that is proven by what I have read at the end of the **Bāb al-Buyū'**. He was humbly in prayers before God, eyes covered with tears, isolated from any company and nothing around him to turn to. It is written in prose and is considered as consisting of ten volumes. I have seen his **Sharḥ al-Siyar al-Kabīr** which is in two volumes. He dictated it while he was in the prison. When he reached the chapter Shurūṭ, he was released from his confinement and was set free. In the last days of his life, he went to Farghāna and came to the palace of Amīr Ḥasan. His students gathered around him and he gave them dictation in the anteroom of the Amīr's palace. The author of the **Masālik** says that while Sarakhsī was held in the prison because of the statement of his advice to the ruler, he wrote his **Kitāb al-Mabsūṭ** in fourteen volumes by giving dictation from his memory without studying or referring to any reading material. I am told that he dictated it to his students from the pit, while they stood above it and wrote it down until it was finished. The **Sharḥ Mukhtaṣar al-Ṭaḥāwī** which I have read in parts and the **Kitāb al-Kasab** which is a small volume, belong to Muḥammad bin Ḥasan (al-Shaybānī). I am told about the gift of his (Sarakhsī's) memory. It is described in the **Masālik** that the ruler married a female slave (umm al-walad) belonging to one of his servants and sought advice regarding the matter from the scholars of his time. They said "it is the best what you did." Shama al-A'imma (Sarakhsī) said it was wrong, because it is considered in the manner of marrying her (slave woman) as a free person. Thereupon, the Amīr said, "I set them free so that the contract of marriage could be renewed," and asked the scholars to give their opinion. They said, "it was best what you did," but Shams al-A'imma said it was wrong (invalid), because (in this case) the waiting period becomes incumbent on the slave mother after being emancipated. During that period, the marriage of Amīr with her is considered as not being valid.

E. TRANSLATED FROM **SHARḤ AL-SIYAR AL-KABĪR** (HYDERABAD EDITION):[10]

It (imprisonment) began on Friday, the third of the month Jumādā al-ūlā in the year 480 A.H./1087 A.D. He (Sarakhsī) began the dictation of his **Sharḥ al-Siyar al-Kabīr** in the prison at Ūzgand. When he reached the chapter al-Shurūṭ he was released from the confinement and he left Ūzgand on Saturday at the end of the month of Rabī al-Awwal in the year 480 A.H./1087 A.D. and came to Marghīnān on Wednesday, the tenth of the month Rabī al-Ākhir and reached the house of Ṣayfuddīn bin Ibrāhīm bin Isḥāq bin Ismā'īl so that he could finish his book. He began with the chapter al-Shurūṭ at his house on the fourteenth of the month Rabī al-Ākhir and finished it on Friday, the third of the month of Jumādā al-ūlā of the year 480 A.H./1087 A.D.

F. TRANSLATED FROM **FAHĀRIS AL-MABSŪṬ** OF SHAMS AL-DĪN AL-SARAKHSĪ BY KHALĪL MAYS:[11]

Sarakhsī's Lineage and Origin:

His name is Muḥammad bin Aḥmad Abū Sahal and agnomen Abū Bakr. Shams al-A'imma Sarakhsī belongs to the Ḥanafī school of thought and was one of the most eminent among the greatest scholars. He was an Imām, a scholar and authority who discussed critically the principles of Islamic jurisprudence with the vision of an original thinker.

His Teachers:

He studied with Imām Shams al-A'imma 'Abd al-'Azīz al-Ḥalwānī (448 A.H./1056 A.D.) until he was certified by him and got the title. He became an exemplary of his time, unsurpassed among his contemporaries.

His Students:

Abū Bakr Muḥammad bin Ibrāhīm al-Ḥuṣayrī (500 A.H./1106 A.D.), Abū 'Omar 'Othmān bin 'Alī al-Baykandī, Abū Ḥafṣ bin Ḥabīb, the grandson from mother's side of the author of the **Hidāya**, the undaunted A'imma 'Abd al-'Azīz bin 'Omar Māza, Maḥmūd bin 'Abd al-'Azīz Ūzgandī and Ruknuddīn Mas'ūd bin Ḥasan studied Islamic jurisprudence under him.

His Stature in the Knowledge (of Jurisprudence):

He made an enemy of Kamāl Pāsha in the juristic matters of giving an independent opinion of which we have no account from his contemporaries, but nonetheless, he reached the status of Abū Bakr al-Khaṣṣāf, Abū Ja'far al-Ṭaḥāwī, Abū Ḥasan al-Karkhī, Pazdawī and others. And the stature he has reached is of those who are the associates of Abū Ḥanīfa in the exercise of legal reasoning. He was, without any dispute, one of the greatest scholars from Transoxiana.

His Writings:

He wrote concerning the Islamic jurisprudence (fiqh) and its principles (uṣūl). He dictated his **Mabsūṭ**, a task of great undertaking. We have written its preface and compiled the index. He wrote it while he was in the prison at Ūzgand which is in Transoxiana in the vicinity of Farghāna. He was confined in the prison due to his advice to the ruler. He dictated it from his memory, without having any books at his disposal, to those in his company (students) standing above the pit. He finished it in the year 477 A.H./1084 A.D.

When he was released, he went to Marghinān in the month of Rabī al-Awwal of the year 480 A.H./1087 A.D. His students flocked around him and he finished the remaining dictation with them. To him also belongs the **Kitab al-Uṣūl**, which consist of two volumes. He also dictated the **Sharḥ al-Siyar** of Muḥammad bin Ḥasan al-Shaybānī, which consists of two thick volumes. To him belongs the **Sharḥ al-Nufaqāt** of Khaṣṣāf and also the **Sharḥ Ādāb al-Qāḍī**. To him also belong the **Ashraṭ al-Sa'āt, Fawā'id al-Faqihā and Kitāb al-Ḥayḍ**, as (mentioned) in the **Kashf al-Ẓunūn**[12].

G. TRANSLATED FROM THE **SHARḤ AL-SIYAR AL-KABĪR** (CAIRO EDITION), ED. BY ṢALĀḤŪDDĪN MUNAJJID:[13]

We do not know much about the life of al-Sarakhsī (Muḥammad ibn Aḥmad bin Sahal Abū Bakr Shams al-A'imma) and that is because he lived too far in Transoxiana and passed his life in confinement, completely cut off from others. What we know of is that he was from Sarakhs (S-R-Khs), which is an ancient city between Mashhad and Marw. He studied Islamic jurisprudence with 'Abd al-'Azīz al-Ḥalwānī who died in the year 448 A.H./1056 A.D. and was certified by him. He excelled in the knowledge of Islamic jurisprudence (fiqh), scholastic philosophy (kalām), principles (uṣūl) of Islamic jurisprudence and disputations (munāẓara) in these matters. Abū Bakr al-Ḥuṣayrī Muḥammad bin Ibrāhīm, who died in 500 A.H./1106 A.D., was one of his students and was certified by him.

Thereafter, he moved to Ūzgand, which is a city in Transoxiana in the neighborhood of Farghāna and came to the palace of the ruler, but soon he was thrown into the prison in the year 466 A.H./1073 A.D., because he gave a juristic opinion that since the slave woman was emancipated, the marriage of the ruler with her was considered as being unlawful before the expiration of the waiting period (from her previous husband). He finished the sentence of imprisonment which lasted for about fifteen years at Ūzgand. The students flocked together, came and took lessons from him in the prison. He dictated books concerning the jurisprudence (fiqh) to them. During the period of his imprisonment, the Imām dictated the **Mabsūṭ** which consists of twenty five volumes from his memory and without referring to any books. He points out that he finished the dictation while he was being held in the prison. He finished the (dictation of) **Mabsūṭ** in the year 477 A.H./1084 A.D.

ENDNOTES

INTRODUCTION

1. See **The Encyclopaedia of Islam**, Vol. II (Leiden: E.J. Brill, 1965), p. 886.

2. See Joseph Schacht, **The Origins of Muhammadan Jurisprudence** (London: Oxford University Press, 1960). Schacht translates the term qiyās as the systematic reasoning throughout the entire text.

3. Ibid., p. 159.

4. See **Shorter Encyclopaedia of Islam** (Ithaca, New York: Cornell University Press, 1965), p. 267.

5. Ibid., p. 104.

6. See **The Encyclopaedia of Islam,** Vol. II (Leiden: E.J. Brill, 1965), p. 888.

7. See **The Shorter Encyclopaedia of Islam** (Ithaca, New York: Cornell University Press, 1965), p. 105.

8. Ibid.

9. Ibid.

10. Sarakhsī, **Mabsūṭ**, Vol. X (Beirut: Dār al- Ma'ārif, 1324-31 A.H./1906-12 A.D.), p. 2.

11. Ibid., p. 145

12. See Sarakhsī **Sharḥ al-Sayir al-Kabīr**, Vol. V (Cairo: Dār al-Ma'ārif, 1908-13) p. 1799; Vol. IV (Hyderabad: Dā'irā al-Ma'ārif, 1335-36 A.H./1916-17 A.D.), p. 73.

13. See Majid Khadduri, **The Islamic Law of Nations, Shaybānī's Siyar** (Baltimore: John Hopkins Press, 1966), pp. 8-9.

14. See Joseph Schacht, **An Introduction to Islamic Law** (Oxford: Oxford University Press, 1966), p. 200.

15. Ibid., p. 204.

16. Sarakhsī, **Mabsūṭ**, Vol. X, (Beirut: Dār al-Ma'ārif, 1324-31 A.H./1906-12 A.D.), p. 145.

CHAPTER ONE

1. It is an old town between Mashhad and Marw where the frontier between modern Asia and Russia turns from east to south. The town is not much of importance. See **The Encyclopaedia of Islam,** Vol. IV (Leiden: E.J.Brill, 1934), p. 159.

2. 'Abd al-Ḥaiy Laknawī, **Kitāb al-Fawā'id al-Bahīya fī Tarājim al-Ḥanafīya** (Cairo: Printed by Aḥmad Nāgī al-Jamālī and Amīn Khānjī, 1914), p. 158.

3. Ibid., 159.

4. Ibn Quṭlūbughā, **Tāj al-Tarājim fī Ṭabqāt**, (Baghdad: Maktaba al-Muthanna, 1962), p. 53.

5. Ḥājī Khalīfa, **Kashf al-Ẓunūn** (Istambul: Maarif Matbassi, 1943), p. 104.

6. 'Abd al-Ḥaiy Laknawī, **Kitāb al-Fawā'id al-Bahīya fī Tarājim al-Ḥanafīya** (Cairo: Printed by Aḥmad al-Jamālī and Amīn Khānjī, 1914), p. 159.

7. Ibid.

8. Ibid., and **Sharḥ al-Sayir al-Kabīr**, Vol. IV (Hyderabad: Dā'īrā al-Ma'ārif, 1908-13), p. 16.

9. Ibn Quṭlūbughā, **Tāj al-Tarājim fī Ṭabqāt al-Ḥanafīya**, (Baghdad: Maktaba al-Muthanna, 1962), p.54.

10. See Ṣalāḥuddīn Munajjid, ed. **Sharḥ al-Siyar al-Kabīr**, Vol. I (Cairo: Dār al-Ma'ārif, 1908-13), p. 16.

11. See **Encyclopaedia of Islam**, Vol. IV (Leiden: E.J. Brill, 1934), p. 159.

12. 'Abd al-Ḥaiy Laknawī, **Kitāb al-Fawā'id al-Bahīya fī Tarājim al-Ḥanafīya** (Cairo: Printed by Aḥmad Nāgī al-Jamālī and Amīn Khānjī, 1914), p. 158.

13. Compare the narration from **Sharḥ al-Sayir al-Kabīr**, Vol.V (Cairo: Dār al-Ma'ārif, (1908-13), p. 1694 and pp. 2293-95; Vol. IV (Hyderabad: Dā'irā al-Ma'rif, 1335-36 A.H./1916-17 A.D.), p. 5 and pp. 384-85 with the Text of Wāqidī's **al-Maghāzī**, Vol. II, ed. M. Jones (London: Oxford University Press), p. 478 and pp. 802-805.

14. **Al-Nukat** lil Imām al-A'imma al-Sarakhsī wa huwa **Sharḥ li Ziyādāt** (Hyderabad: Dār al Ma'ārif, 1378 A.H./1958 A.D.).

15. See the title of Schacht's **Das Kitāb al-Makhārij fī al-Ḥiyal** des Imām Muḥammad bin al-Shaybānī wa yalbahu riwāya li hadhā al-Kitāb li Shams al-A'imma Abī Bakr Muḥammad bin Aḥmad bin Abī Sahal al-Sarakhsī (namely, there is another narration of this book written by Sarakhsī), (Leipzig: J.C. Heinrich's Buchhandlung, 1930).

16. Joseph Schacht, **Abhandlungen der Preussichen Akademie der Wissenschaften** (Berlin, Verlag der Akademie der Wissenschaften, 1930), p. 6. Schacht also describes here the condition and summary contents of the manuscripts of the said work found in various libraries. But, from this it would be difficult to ascertain anything definite, as to whether Sarakhsī is representing in this work his own views or the views of Shaybānī and Aḥmad al-Marawazī al-Ḥakīm al-Shahīd.

17. Ḥājī Khalīfa, **Kashf al-Ẓunūn** (Istambul: Maarif Matbassi, 1943), p. 1298 and p. 1414.

18. Ibn Quṭlūbughā, **Tāj al-Tarājim fī Ṭabqāt al-Ḥanafīya** (Baghdad: Maktaba al-Muthanna, 1962), p. 54.

19. Ḥājī Khalīfa, **Kashf al-Ẓunūn** (Istambul: Maarif Matbassi, 1943), p. 46.

20. Ṣalāḥuddīn Munnajid, **Sharḥ al-Siyar al-Kabīr**, Vol. I (Cairo: Dār al-Ma'ārif, 1908-13), p. 17.

CHAPTER TWO

1. See **Shorter Encyclopaedia of Islam** (Ithaca, New York: Cornell University Press, 1965), p. 105.

2. Joseph Schacht, **The Origins of Muhammadan Jurisprudence** (London: Oxford University Press, 1950); Ignaz Goldziher, "Das Princip des Istiṣḥāb in der muhammedanischen Geseztwissenschaft," **Gesammelte Schriften**, Band II (Hildesheim: George Olms, 1967), p. 182.

3. Joseph Schacht, **Origins of Muhammadan Jurisprudence** (London: Oxford University Press, 1950), p. 182.

4. Abū Yūsuf, **Kitāb al-Kharāj** (Cairo: Būlāq, 1884), p. 108.

5. Ibid.

6. Ibid.

7. Ibid., p. 112.

8. Ibid., p. 117.

9. See Ibid., on the margin p. 119.

10. Joseph Schacht, **Origins of Muhammadan Jurisprudence** (London: Oxford University Press, 1950), p. 307.

11. Khalīl Mays, **Fahāris al-Mabsūṭ** (Beirut: Dār al-Ma'ārif, 1980), p. 10.

12. Ibid., p. 7.

13. Ḥājī Khalīfa, **Kashf al-Ẓunūn** (Istambul: Maarif Matbassi, 1943), p. 43.

14. See, for example, Sarakhsī, **Sharḥ al-Siyar al-Kabīr**, Vol. V (Cairo: Dār al-Ma'ārif, 1908), p. 1713, 1922 and 2077; Vol. IV (Hyderabad: Dā'irā al-Ma'ārif, 1335-36 A.H./1916-17 A.D.), p. 18, 129 and 2077.

15. See, for example, Sarakhsī, **Sharḥ al-Siyar al-Kabīr**, Vol. V (Cairo: Dār al-Ma'ārif,1908), pp. 2151, pp. 2232-33; Vol. IV (Hyderabad: Dā'irā al-Ma'ārif, 1335-36 A.H./1916- 7 A.D.), p. 294, 346 and also Sarakhsī, **Uṣūl al-Sarakhsī**, ed. Abū al-Wafā al-Afghānī: Lajnat Iḥyā al-Ma'ārif al-Nu'mānīya, 1954), p. 254.

16. See Muḥammad bin Ḥasan al-Shaybānī, **Kitāb al-Aṣl (Bāb al-Istiḥsān)**, ed. Abū al-Wafā al-Afghānī, Vol. III, Part II (Hyderabad: Dā'irā al-Ma'ārif, 1335-36 A.H./1916-17 A.D.), p. 2.

17. See Sarakhsī, **Mabsūṭ**, Vol. X (Beirut: Dār al-Ma'ārif, 1324-31/1906-31), pp. 2-3.

18. Ṣalāḥuddīn Munajjid, ed. **Sharḥ al-Siyar al-Kabīr**, Vol. I (Cairo: Dār al-Ma'ārif, 1908-13), pp. 17.

19. Sarakhsī, **Mabsūṭ**, Vol. X (Beirut: Dār al-Ma'ārif, 1324-31), p. 2.

20. Ibid., pp. 2-3.

21. Sarakhsī, **Sharḥ al-Siyar al-Kabīr**, Vol. V (Cairo: Dār al-Ma'ārif, 1908), p. 2210; Vol. IV (Hyderabad: Dā'irā al-Ma'ārif, 1335-36 A.H./1916-17), p. 332.

22. Ibid., (Cairo edition), p. 2282; (Hyderabad edition), p. 378.

23. Ibid., (Cairo edition), p. 1816; (Hyderabad edition), p. 84.

24. See Hans Kruse, "The Foundation of Islamic International Jurisprudence (Muḥammad al-Shaybani-Hugo Grotius of the Muslims)," **Pakistan Historical Society Journal**, Vol. III, Part IV, 1955, pp. 20-27.

25. Hans Kruse, "The Foundation of Islamic International Jurisprudence (Muḥammad al-Shaybani-Hugo Grotius of the Muslims)," **Pakistan Historical Society Journal**, Vol. III, Part IV, 1955, p. 31.

CHAPTER THREE

1. Sarakhsī, **Mabsūṭ**, Vol. X (Beirut: Dār al-Ma'ārif, 1324-31 A.H./1906-12 A.D.), p. 145.

2. Ibid.

3. Sūra II, 185.

4. Bukharī, Imān 34.

5. Sarakhsī, **Uṣūl al-Sarakhsī**, Vol. II ed. Abū al-Wafā al-Afghānī, (Cairo: Lajnat Iḥyā al-Ma'ārif al- Nu'mānīya, 1954), p. 130.

6. Ibid., pp. 199-223.

7. Ibid., pp. 200-201.

8. Ibid., p. 201.

9. Sarakhsī, **Mabsūṭ**, Vol. X (Beirut: Dār al-Ma'ārif, 1324-31 A.H./1906-12 A.D.), p. 145.

10. Ibid., p. 145.

11. Sarakhsī, **Uṣūl al-Fiqh**, Vol. II ed. Abū al-Wafā al-Afghānī (Cairo: Lajnat Iḥyā al-Ma'ārif al-Nu'mānīya, 1954), p. 203.

12. Muhammad bin Idrīs Shāfi'ī, **Kitāb al-Umm**, Vol. VII (Cairo: Būlāq 1331 A.H./1968 A.D.), pp. 267-69.

13. Muhammad bin Idrīs Shāfi'ī, **Risāla**, trans. Majid Khadduri, **Islamic Jurisprudence, Shāfi'ī's Risāla** (Baltimore: The John Hopkins Press, 1961), pp. 304-332.

14. Ibid., p. 304.

15. Majid Khadduri, **Islamic Jurisprudence, Shāfi'ī's Risāla** (Baltimore: The John Hopkins Press, 1961), p. 70.

16. See Sarakhsī, **Uṣūl al-Sarakhsī**, Vol. II, ed. Abū al-Wafā al-Afghānī (Cairo: Lajnat Iḥyā al-Ma'ārif al-Nu'mānīya, 1954), p. 140.

17. Majid Khadduri, **Islamic Jurisprudence, Shāfi'ī's Risāla** (Baltimore: The John Hopkins Press, 1961), p. 70.

18. Ibid., pp. 304-305.

19. Ibid., p. 306.

20. Ibid., p. 305.

21. Sarakhsī, **Uṣūl-al Sarakhsī**, Vol. II, ed. Abū al-Wafā al-Afghānī (Cairo: Lajnat Iḥyā al-Ma'ārif al- Nu'mānīya, 1954), pp. 127-129.

22. Ibid., pp. 127-129.

23. Ibid., p. 132.

24. Ibid., p. 138.

25. Ibid., pp. 149-150.

26. Sarakhsī, **Sharḥ al-Sayīr al-Kabīr**, Vol. V (Cairo: Dār al-Ma'ārif, 1908) p. 2039; Vol. IV (Hyderabad: Dā'irā al-Ma'ārif, 1335-36 A.H./1916-17), p. 335.

27. Ibid. (Cairo edition), p. 1816; (Hyderabad edition), p. 84.

28. Ibid.

29. Ibid. (Cairo edition), p. 1813; (Hyderabad edition), p. 82.

30. Ibid.

31. Joseph Schacht, **Origins of Muhammadan Jurisprudence** (London: Oxford University Press, 1960), p. 298.

32. Sarakhsī, **Sharḥ al-Siyar al-Kabīr**, Vol. V (Cairo: Dār al-Ma'ārif, 1908), p. 1900; Vol. IV (Hyderabad: Dā'irā al-Ma'ārif, 1335-36 A.H./ 1916-17), p. 138.

33. Ibid. (Cairo edition), p. 1885; (Hyderabad edition), p. 129.

34. Ibid. (Cairo edition), p. 1725; (Hyderabad edition) p. 25.

35. Ibid. (Cairo edition), p. 1857; (Hyderabad edition), p. 111.

36. Ibid. (Cairo edition), p. 2196; (Hyderabad edition) p. 322.

37. Ibid. (Cairo edition), p. 1861; (Hyderabad edition), p. 113.

38. Ibid. (Cairo edition), p. 1900; (Hyderabad edition), p. 139.

39. Ibid. (Cairo edition), p. 1739, 1741; (Hyderabad edition), p. 35, 36.

40. Ibid. (Cairo edition), p. 1790; (Hyderabad edition), p. 67.

41. Ibid. (Cairo edition), p. 2135; (Hyderabad edition), p. 284.

42. Ibid. (Cairo edition), p. 1790; (Hyderabad edition), p. 67.

43. Ibid. (Cairo edition), p. 2139; (Hyderabad edition), p. 285.

44. Ibid. (Cairo edition), p.1803; (Hyderabad edition), p. 75.

45. Ibid. (Cairo edition), p. 1725; (Hyderabad edition), p. 25.

46. Ibid. (Cairo edition), p. 1803; (Hyderabad edition), p. 25.

47. Ibid. (Cairo edition), p. 1713, 1719; (Hyderabad edition), p. 17, 21.

48. Ibid. (Cairo edition), p. 1689, 1694, 1724; (Hyderabad edition), p. 2, 5, 24.

CHAPTER FOUR

1. Sarakhsī, **Uṣūl al-Sarakhsī**, Vol. II, ed. Abū al-Wafā al-Afghānī (Cairo: Lajnat Iḥyā al-Ma'ārif al-Nu'mānīya, 1954), p. 217.

2. Ibid., p. 221.

3. Ibid., p. 238.

4. Ibid., p. 239.

5. Ibid., p. 240.

6. Ibid., p. 240.

7. Ibid., p. 241.

8. Ibid., p. 242.

9. Ibid.

10. Ibid.

11. Ibid., p. 243.

12. Ibid.

13. Ibid.

14. Ibid., pp. 243-244.

15. Ibid., p. 250.

16. Ibid., p. 253.

17. Ibid., p. 254.

18. Ibid., pp. 258-259.

19. Ibid., p. 261.

20. Ibid.

21. Ibid., p. 262.

22. Ibid., p. 264.

23. Ibid., pp. 254-255.

24. Ibid., p. 265.

25. Ibid.

CHAPTER FIVE

1. See Majid Khadduri, **The Islamic Law of Nations, Shaybānī's Siyar** (Baltimore: The John Hopkins Press, 1966), p. 8-9.

2. Ibid., p. 145.

3. Shaybānī, **Jāmi' al-Ṣaghīr**, printed on the margin of Abū Yūsuf's **Kitāb al-Kharāj** (Cairo: Būlāq, 1302 A.H./1884 A.D.), pp. 103-104.

4. See Majid Khadduri, **The Islamic Law of Nations, Shaybānī's Siyar** (Baltimore: The John Hopkins University Press, 1966), p. 44.

5. See Hans Kruse, "The Foundation of Islamic International Jurisprudence (Muḥammad al-Shaybānī-Hugo Grotius of the Muslims), **Pakistan Historical Society Journal**, Vol. III, Part IV, 1955, p. 31.

6. See Majid Khadduri, **The Islamic Law of Nations, Shaybānī's Siyar** (Baltimore: The John Hopkins Press, 1966), p. 116.

7. Sarakhsī, **Uṣūl al-Sarakhsī**, Vol. II, ed. Abū al-Wafā al-Afghanī (Cairo: Lajnat Iḥyā al-Ma'ārif al-Nu'māniya, 1954), pp. 220-221.

8. See Majid Khadduri, **The Islamic Law of Nations, Shaybānī's Siyar** (Baltimore: The John Hopkins University Press, 1966), p. 167.

9. Sarakhsī, **Mabsūṭ**, Vol. X (Beirut: Dār al-Ma'ārif, 1324-31 A.H./ 1906-12 A.D.), p. 91.

10. Ibid., pp. 70-71.

11. See Majid Khadduri, **The Islamic Law of Nations, Shaybānī's Siyar** (Baltimore: The John Hopkins University Press, 1966), p. 75.

12. Ibid., pp. 142-156.

13. Sarakhsī, **Mabsūṭ**, Vol. X (Beirut: Dār al-Ma'ārif, 1324-31 A.H./1906-12 A.D.), p. 85.

14. Sarakhsī, **Sharḥ al-Siyar al-Kabīr**, Vol. V (Cairo: Dār al-Ma'ārif, 1971), p. 1788; Vol. IV (Hyderabad: Dā'rā al-Ma'ārif, 1335-36/1916-17), p. 66.

15. Ibid. (Cairo edition), p. 1780; (Hyderabad edition), p. 60.

16. Ibid. (Cairo edition), p. 1781; (Hyderabad edition), p. 61.

17. Ibid. (Cairo edition), p. 1781-82; (Hyderabad edition), p. 61-62.

18. Ibid. (Cairo edition), p. 1782; (Hyderabad edition), p. 62.

19. Ibid. (Cairo edition), p. 1801; (Hyderabad edition), p. 74.

20. Ibid. (Cairo edition), p. 1819; (Hyderabad edition), p. 86.

21. Ibid. (Cairo edition), p. 1816; (Hyderabad edition), p. 84.

22. Ibid. (Cairo edition), p. 1941; (Hyderabad edition), p. 164.

23. Ibid. (Cairo edition), p. 1816; (Hyderabad edition), p. 84.

24. Ibid. (Cairo edition), p. 1813; (Hyderabad edition), p. 82.

25. Ibid.

26. See Majid Khadduri, **The Islamic Law of Nations, Shaybānī's Siyar** (Baltimore: The John Hopkins University Press, 1966), pp. 130-139.

27. Sarakhsī, **Sharḥ al-Siyar al-Kabīr**, Vol. V (Cairo: Dār al-Ma'ārif, 1971), p. 1900; Vol. IV (Dār al-Ma'ārif, 1335-36 A.H./1916-17), p. 66.

28. Ibid. (Cairo edition), p. 1725; Hyderabad edition, p. 25.

29. Ibid. (Cairo edition), p. 2196; (Hyderabad edition), p. 322.

30. Ibid.

31. Ibid. (Cairo edition), p. 1861; (Hyderabad edition), p. 113.

32. Ibid. (Cairo edition), p. 1788; (Hyderabad edition), p. 66.

33. Ibid. (Cairo edition), p. 1745; (Hyderabad edition), p. 39.

34. See Majid Khadduri, **The Islamic Law of Nations, Shaybānī's Siyar** (Baltimore: The John Hopkins University Press), pp. 174-175.

35. Sarakhsī, **Sharḥ al-Siyar al-Kabīr**, Vol. V (Cairo: Dār al-Ma'ārif, 1971), p. 1970; Vol. IV (Dā'irā al-Ma'ārif, 1335-36 A.H./1916-17), p. 66.

36. Ibid. (Cairo edition), p. 1713, 1721, 1803; (Hyderabad edition), p. 17, 22, 75.

37. Ibid. (Cairo edition), p. 1721; (Hyderabad edition), p. 22.

38. Ibid. (Cairo edition), pp. 2-3; (Hyderabad edition), pp. 85-86.

39. Ibid. (Cairo edition), p. 1891; (Hyderabad edition), p. 133.

40. Ibid. (Cairo edition), pp. 2223-24; (Hyderabad edition), pp. 341-42.

41. Ibid.

CHAPTER SIX

1. See **Shorter Encyclopaedia of Islam**, (Ithaca, New York: Cornell University Press, 1965), pp. 104-105.

2. Ibid., p. 105.

3. Ibid.

4. Ibid., p. 185.

5. Ibid., p. 105.

6. Ibid.

7. Ibid.; See also Ignaz Goldziher, "Das Princip des Istiṣḥāb in Muḥammedanischen Gesetszwissenschaft," **Gesammelte Schriften**, Band II (Hildesheim: G. Olms Verlags Buchhandlung, 1968), p. 185 and pp.188-89.

8. See **The Encyclopaedia of Islam**, Vol. IV (Leiden: E.J. Brill, 1978), p. 258.

9. See **Shorter Encyclopaedia of Islam** (Ithaca, New York: Cornell Univeristy Press, 1965), p. 185.

10. Ibid., pp. 185-86.

11. Ibid., p. 185.

12. Pazdawī, **Kashf al-Asrār ʻan Uṣūl Fakhr al-Islām al-Bazdawī**, Commentary by ʻAbd al-ʻAzīz bin Aḥmad al-Bukhārī, Part IV (Beirut: Dār al-ʻArabī, 1974), p. 3.

13. Ibid.

14. Ibid.; See also Nicholas F.Aghnides, **Mohammadan Theories of Finance with an Introduction to Muhammadan Law and a Bibliography** (AMS Press, New York, 1969), p. 98.

15. Ibid.

16. Ibid.

17. Ibid.

18. ʻAbd Allah ibn Aḥmad al-Nasafī, **Manār al-Anwār, Manẓūmāt al-Kawākibī**, (Cairo: Maṭbaʻa al-ʻIlmīya, 1317 A.H.), p. 78.

19. Ibid., p. 76.

20. Ibid., p. 83.

21. Ibid., p. 83.

22. Ibid., p. 73.

23. Ibid., p. 76.

24. See **Encyclopaedia of Islam**, Supplement, Fascieules 1-2 (Leiden: E.J. Brill, 1980), p. 25.

25. Abū al-Ḥusayn al-Baṣrī, **Kitāb al-Mu'tamad fī Uṣūl al-Fiqh** (Damascus: Institute Français De Dame, 1964), pp. 838-39.

26. Ibid., p. 839.

27. Ibid., p. 840.

28. Ibid.

29. Abū Ḥāmid Muḥammad Ghazālī, **Al-Mustaṣfā min al-Uṣūl**, Vol. I (Baghdad: Muthannā, 1970), p. 315. See also Muhammad Khalid Masud, **Islamic Legal Philosophy**, (Islamabad: Islamic Research Institute, 1977), pp. 154-56. Masud has expounded on this aspect of Ghazālī's thought at great length. Here only the most important points relevant to the doctrine of istiḥsān are reproduced summarily.

30. Ibid., pp. 294-95; p. 177.

31. Muhammad Khalid Masud, **Islamic Legal Philosophy** (Islamabad: Islamic Research Institute, 1977), P. 155.

32. Ibid., p. 155.

33. Ibid., p. 156.

34. Abū Ḥāmid Muḥammad Ghazālī, **Al-Mustaṣfā min al-Uṣūl**, Vol. I (Baghdad: Muthannā, 1970), p. 274

35. Muhammad Khalid Masud, **Islamic Legal Philosophy**, (Islamabad: Islamic Research Institute, 1977), p. 158.

36. Ibid.

37. Ibid., pp. 158-59.

38. Jamāl al-Dīn Isnawī, **Nihāyat al-Su'al**, printed on the margin of Amīr al-Ḥājj, **Al-Taqrīr wa al-Taḥbīr** (Cairo: Bulāq, 1317 A.H./1899 A.D.), p. 136.

39. Muhammad Khalid Masud, **Islamic Legal Philosophy** (Islamabad: Islamic Research Institute, 1977), p. 161.

40. Jamāl al-Dīn Isnawī, **Nihāyat al-Su'al**, printed on the margin of Amīr al-Ḥājj, **Al-Taqrīr wa al-Taḥbīr** (Cairo: Būlāq, 1317 A.H./1917 A.D.), p. 136.

41. Ibid., p. 140.

42. Ibid., p. 140.

43. Ibid., p. 146.

44. Ibid.

45. Ibid.

46. Sarakhsī, **Uṣūl al-Sarakhsī**, Vol. II, ed. Abū al-Wafā al-Afghānī (Cairo: Lajnat: Iḥyā al-Ma'ārif, 1954), p. 250.

47. Tāj al-Dīn Subkī, **Jāmi' al-Jawāmi'**, Vol. II, printed on the margin of 'Abd al-Raḥmān Bannānī. . . . **'alā matn Jāwāmī'** (Cairo: Muṣṭafā Bābī, 1937), p. 263.

48. Ibid., pp. 266-67.

49. Sura II, 222.

50. Tāj al-Dīn Subkī, **Jāmi' al-Jawāmi'**, Vol. II, printed on the margin of 'Abd al-Raḥmān Bannānī. . . . . **'alā matn Jāmi' al-Jawāmi'** (Cairo: Muṣṭafā Bābī, 1937), pp. 267-68.

51. Sūra LXVII, 9.

52. Tāj al-Dīn Subkī, **Jāmi' al-Jawāmi'**, Vol. II, Printed on the margin of 'Abd al-Raḥmān al-Bannānī. . . . **'alā matn Jāmi' al-Jawāmi'** (Cairo: Muṣṭafā Bābī, 1937), p. 270.

53. Ibid., p. 284.

54. Ibid., p. 282.

55. Ibid., p. 284.

56. Ibid., p. 267.

57. See George Makdisi, "Ibn Taimiya's Autograph Manuscript on Istiḥsān," **Materials for the Study of Islamic Legal Thought in Arabic and Islamic Studies in Honor of Hamilton A.H. Gibb** (Leiden: E.J. Brill, 1965), p. 448.

58. Ibid., p. 447.

59. Aḥmad ibn al-Ḥalīm Taymīya, **Majmū'āt al-Rasā'il wa al-Masā'il**, Vol. V (Cairo: Maṭba'a al-Manār, 1349 A.H./1930 A.D.), p. 22.

60. Ibid., p. 23.

61. Ibid.

62. Ibid.

63. Ibid.

64. Ibid.

65. Ibid.

66. Ibid.

67. Mas'ūd ibn 'Omar al-Taftāzānī, **Sharḥ al-Talwīḥ 'alā al-Tawḍīḥ** (al-Talwīḥ, **Commentary** by Taftāzānī), Vol. I (Cairo: Būlāq, Maktaba al-Kubrīya al-Amīrīya, 1318 A.H./1900 A.D.), p. 117.

68. Ibid.

69. Ibid., p. 79.

70. Ibid., p. 23.

71. Ibid., p 94.

72. Ibid., p. 103.

73. Ibid., p. 82.

74. Sarakhsī, **Uṣūl al-Sarakhsī**, ed. Abū al-Wafā al-Afghānī (Cairo: Lajnat al-Iḥyā al-Ma'ārif, 1372 A.H./1954 A.D.), p. 250.

75. Ibid.

76. Ibid., pp. 115-16.

77. Ibid., p. 99.

78. Ibid., p. 117.

79. Ibid.

80. See Muḥammad Sa'īd Ramḍān Būṭī, **Ḍawābiṭ al-Maṣlaḥa fī al-Sharī'a al-Islāmīya** (Damascus: al-Maktaba al-Umawīya, 1966-67), pp. 202-215.

81. Sarakhsī, **Uṣūl al-Sarakhsī**, Vol. II, ed. Abū al-Wafā al-Afghanī (Cairo: Lajnat Iḥyā al-Ma'ārif, 1954), pp. 138-39.

82. Muḥammad Sa'īd Ramḍān Būṭī, **Ḍawābiṭ al-Maṣlaḥa fī al-Sharī'a al-Islāmīya** (Damascus: al-Maktaba al-Umawīya, 1966-67), p. 240.

83. Ibid., p. 241.

84. Sarakhsī, **Sharh al-Siyar al-Kabīr**, Vol. V. (Cairo: Lajnat, Dār al-Ma'ārif, 1908), p. 2091; Vol. IV (Hyderabad: Dā'irā al-Ma'ārif, 1335-36 A.H./1916-17 A.D.), p. 253.

85. Sarakhsī, **Uṣūl al-Sarakhsī**, Vol. II, ed. Abā al-Wafā al-Afghanī (Cairo: Lajnat Iḥyā al-Ma'ārif al-Nu'mānīya, 1954), p. 259.

86. Muḥammad Sa'īd Ramḍān, **Ḍawābiṭ al-Maṣlaḥa fī al-Sharī' al-Islamīya** (Damascus: al-Maktaba al-Umawīya, 1966-67), pp. 244-45.

87. 'Izz al-Dīn 'Abd al-Salām Sulmī, **Qawā'id al-Aḥkām fī Maṣāliḥ al-Anām**, Vol. I (Cairo: Maktaba al-Kulliyāt al-Azharīya, 1969), p. 11.

88. See Muhammad Khalid Masud, **Islamic Legal Philosophy** (Islamabad: Islamic research Institute, 1977), p. 161.

89. 'Izz al-Dīn 'Abd al-Salām Sulmī, **Qawā'id al-Aḥkām fī Maṣāliḥ al-Anām**, Vol. I (Cairo: Maktaba al-Kulliyāt al-Azharīya, 1969), p. 10.

90. Ibid.

91. Ibid., pp. 11-12.

92. Ibid., p. 10.

93. Ibid., p. 31.

94. Shihāb al-Dīn Qarāfī, **Tanqīḥ al-Fuṣūl fī Ikhtiṣār al-Maḥṣūl fī al-Uṣūl** (Cairo: Maktaba al-Kullīyāt al-Azharīa, 1961), p. 451.

95. Ibid., p. 418; see also Muhammad Khalid Masud, **Islamic Legal Philosophy** (Islamabad: Islamic Research Institute, 1977), p. 235.

96. Shihāb al-Dīn Qarāfī, **Tanqīḥ al-Fuṣūl fī Ikhtiṣār al-Maḥṣūl** (Cairo: Maktaba al-Kullīyāt al-Azharīya, 1961), p. 45.

97. Ibid., p. 413.

98. Ibid., pp. 394-95.

99. Ibid., p. 420.

100. Ibid., p. 441.

101. Ibid.

102. Ibid., p. 447.

103. Ignaz Goldziher, **Streitschrift des Ghazālī gegen des Bāṭinijja-Sekte** (Leiden: E. J. Brill, 1961), pp. 32-34.

104. Muhammad Khalid Masud, **Islamic Legal Philosophy** (Islamabad: Islamic Research Institute, 1977), p. 194.

105. Ibid., p. 322.

106. Ibid., pp. 306-07.

107. Ibid., p. 225. It is to be noted that in the following two paragraphs, the quotations from Shāṭibī's **al-Muwāfqāt** and their summary is reproduced from Muhammad Khalid Masud, **Islamic Legal Philosophy** (Islamabad: Islamic Research Institute, 1977), pp. 225-36.

108. Ibid., pp. 226-27.

109. Ibid., p. 233.

110. See Abū Isḥāq al-Shāṭibī, **Al-I'tiṣām**, Vol. II (Cairo: Maṭba'a al-Manār, 1913), pp. 281-341.

111. Ibid., p. 316.

112. Ibid., p. 317.

113. Ibid., p. 320.

114. Ibid., pp. 330-31.

115. Abū Isḥāq al-Shāṭibī, **Al-I'tiṣām**, Vol. I (Cairo: Maṭba'a al-Manār, 1913), p. 316.

116. Ibid., pp. 314-15.

117. Ibid., p. 315.

118. Ibid., p. 315.

119. Abū Isḥāq al-Shāṭibī, **Al-I'tiṣām**, Vol. II (Cairo: Maṭba'a al-Manār, 1913), p. 316.

120. Ibid., p. 327.

121. Sūra XXXIX, 18.

122. Ibn Ḥazm, **Iḥkām fī Uṣūl al-Aḥkām**, Vol. X, ed. Aḥmad Muḥammad Shākir (Cairo: Maktaba al-Khānjī, 1947), pp. 16-17; see also A.G. Chenje, **Ibn Ḥazm** (Chicago: Kazi Publications, 1982), p. 122.

123. Ibn Ḥazm, **Iḥkām fī Uṣūl al-Aḥkām**, Vol. X, ed. Aḥmad Muḥammad Shākir (Cairo: Maktaba al-Khānjī, 1947), p. 17.

124. Ibid., p. 21.

125. Najm al-Dīn Ṭūfī, "Bayān i'tibār al-Maṣlaḥa al-Aḥkām al-Mu'āmalāt," **Al-Manār,** Vol. IX, p. 752.

126. Quoted after Malcolm Kerr, "Rashid Riḍā and Islamic Legal Reform: An Ideological Analysis, "**The Muslim World,** Vol. L. No. 1, p. 108.

127. Najm al-Dīn Ṭūfī, "Bayān i'tibār al-Maṣlaḥa al-Aḥkām al-Mu'āmalāt," **Al-Manār,** Vol. IX, p. 752.

128. Ibid.

129. Ibid., p. 755.

130. Malcom H. Kerr, **The Political Thought and Legal Theories of Muḥammad 'Abdū and Rashīd Riḍā** (Berkeley: University of California Press, 1966), p. 258.

131. Muhammad Khalid Masud, **Islamic Legal Philosophy** (Islamabad: Islamic Research Institute, 1977), p. 165.

132. Malcolm H. Kerr, **The Political and Legal Theories of Muḥammad 'Abdū and Rashīd Riḍā** (Berkeley: University of California Press, 1966), p. 258.

APPENDIX

1. 'Abd al-Ḥaiy Laknawī, **Kitāb al-Fawā'id al-Bahīya fī al-Tarājim al-Ḥanafīya** (Cairo: Printed by Aḥmad Nāgī al-Jamālī and Amīn Khānjī, 1914), pp. 158-59.

2. Obviously, Laknawī is referring to chapter five of Sarakhsī's **Sharḥ al-Siyar al-Kabīr.**

3. From this it can be concluded that Laknawī maintains Sarakhsī died around 500 A.H./1106 A.D.) and not 490 A.H./1096 A.D. as mentioned in other sources.

4. Obviously, Laknawī is repeating himself. Maybe, he is impressed by the fact that Sarakhsī accomplished such a great task in spite of his being held in the prison.

5. Abū J'afar Aḥmad bin Muḥammad bin Salmān al-Ṭaḥāwī (239 A.H./853 A.D). To him belong **Ma'ānī al-Āthār** and **Bayān al-Mushkil al-Ḥadīth** (also known as **Mushkil al-Āthār**). It is said that he also wrote **Sharḥ** of Shaybānī's **Jāmi' al-Ṣaghīr**. See ed. Muḥammad Ṣaghīr Ḥasan Ma'ṣūmī, **Disagreement of Jurists (Ikhtilāf al-Fuqahā'** (Islamabad: Islamic Research Institute, 1971), pp. 48-49.

6. Ibn Abū al-Wafā Qurashī, **Jawāhir al-Muḍīya**(Hyderabad: Dā'irā al-Ma'ārif, 1980), pp. 191-92.

7. Ḥājī Khalīfa, **Kashaf al-Ẓunūn** (Istambul: Maarif Mathassi, 1943), pp. 1013-14.

8. Ḥājī Khalīfa is commenting at this place on **al-Siyar al-Kabīr and al-Siyar al-Ṣaghīr** presumably written by Shaybānī. As already mentioned in Chapter One, Sarakhsī, among others, wrote **Sharḥ** of **al-Siyar al-Kabīr**. After mentioning this, Ḥājī Khalīfa, continues to describe a few annecdotes about Shaybānī and his work, **al-Siyar al-Kabīr.**

9. Ibn Quṭūbughā, **Tāj al-Tarājim fī Ṭabaqāt al-Ḥanafīya** (Baghdad: Maktaba al-Muthanna, 1962), pp. 53-54.

10. Sarakhsī, **Sharḥ al-Siyar al-Kabīr**, Vol. IV (Hyderabad: Dā'irā al-Ma'ārif, 1335 A.H./1916 A.D.), pp. 386-87.

11. Khalīl Mays, **Fahāris al-Mabsūṭ** (Beirut: Dār al- Ma'ārif, 1980), pp. 7-8.

12. See Ḥājī Khalīfa, **Kashf al-Ẓunūn** (Istambul: Maarif Matbassi, 1943), p. 46.

13. Sarakhsī, **Sharḥ al-Siyar al-Kabīr**, Vol. I, ed. Ṣalāḥuddīn Munajjid (Cairo: Dār al-Ma'ārif, 1324-31 A.H./1908-13 A.D.), p. 16.

GLOSSARY OF ARABIC TECHNICAL TERMS

'ādāt: (sing. 'āda) practices, customs or mores of the people.

'adl: (pl.'udūl) of good and veracious character.

aghrāḍ: (sing. gharaḍ) motives or personal interests.

aḥādīth: (sing.ḥadīth) see ḥadīth.

aḥkām al-ākhira: heareafter affairs.

ahl al-ḥadīth: traditionalists.

ahl al-ra'y: rationalists.

ahwā al-nufūs: see hawā.

ākhira: hereafter.

'amal: act, synonymous with the Sunna, actual practice in Medina.

amān: safe conduct, promise of security.

amāra: sign, indication.

'aql: human reason, intellectual faculty.

aṣl: (pl. uṣūl) here translated as Origin with capital "O", suggesting the root and the source to which the 'illa (effective reasoning) is sought in the doctrine of systematic reasoning (qiyās) and the doctrine of juristic preference (istiḥsān).

athar: evidence.

athār: Antiquity, the authority based on the Prophet's utterances and the Caliph's decisions.

bāṭil: invalid, null and void.

bāṭin: implicit, hidden.

bida'a: innovation.

ḍa'īf: weak.

aḥkām al-dīn: religious affairs.

aḥkām al-dunyā: worldly affairs.

ḍalāl: error.

dalāla: indication.

dalīl: evidence.

dār al-dhimma: territory of protection by the treaty of surrender.

dār al-ḥarb: territory of war.

dār al-ḥarbī: inhabitant of the territory of war.

dār al-Islām: territory or abode of Muslims.

ḍarūra: necessity.

ḍarūrī: necessary.

dhawq: taste, mystic taste.

dhimma: protection.

dhimmī: an inhabitant of the territory protected by a treaty of surrender.

dunyā: this world (as opposed to hereafter (ākhira).

faraḥ: happiness

fāsid: invalid, null and void.

fiqh: the (science of) Islamic jurisprudence.

fuqhā': (pl. of faqīh) jurists or the authorities in the matters of Islamic jurisprudence and sharī'a laws.

furū': the branches of law, as opposed to the uṣūl al-fiqh, principles or roots of Islamic jurisprudence).

gharaḍ: motive or personal interest.

ghulū: exceeding proper bounds of sharī'a.

ghusal: major ritual of ablution i.e. washing of the whole body.

ḥadd: (pl. ḥudūd) the legal punishment prescribed by the sharī'a laws.

ḥadīth: (pl. aḥādīth) the tradition or narration from the Prophet, second source of Islamic jurisprudence after the Qur'ān.

ḥāja: general need.

ḥaq: (pl. ḥuqūq) right.

ḥuqūq al-Allah: rights of God.

ḥuqūq al-'ibād: right of individual human beings.

hawā: passion, desire.

hawā al-nafs: personal liking.

'ibādāt: (pl. of 'ibāda) religious observances.

'idda: waiting period (considered as duration of four months and ten days) to be observed by the woman after termination of marriage.

ijmā': general consensus in the matters of sharī'a laws of the people of the first three successive generations after the death of the Prophet. It is the third source of law in Islamic jurisprudence.

ijtihād: exercise of legal reasoning (ra'y) for the derivation of an indepedent judgment (ḥukm).

Ikhtilāf al-ra'y: differences of opinion among the jurists.

ilghā': null and void.

'illa: effective reasoning employed in the exercise of ra'y (legal reasoning) in the four schools of thought in Islamic jurisprudence in various forms.

imā': implicit indication.

istidlāl: reasoning, proof, evidence.

istidrāk: rectification.

istiḥsān: what is preferable, the doctrine of

juristictic preference in the Ḥanafī school of thought by which a jurist on the basis of legal reasoning (ra'y) favors one judgment (ḥukm) rahter than another which may have been arrived at by the doctrine of qiyās (systematic reasoning).

istiṣlāḥ: taking into consideration of what is beneficial or expedient (maṣlaḥa), the doctrine of juristic reasoning in the Mālikī school of thought on the basis of which a jurist decides in favor of one judgment rather than another which may have been arrived at by the doctrine of qiyās (systematic reasoning).

istiṣḥāb: the presumption of continuity of juristic or legal situation as it had existed previously, so long as there does not exist any evidence for its discontinuity; a method of legal reasoning (ra'y) exercised in the Shāfi'ī school of thought.

istithnā': exception.

istinbāṭ: inference.

jalīy: evident, explicit.

jins: sameness of things.

jins al-aḥkām: sameness of judgments.

jizya: poll tax.

kashf: mystic revelation.

khabar: narrative from the Text of the Qur'ān or Sunna

kharāj: land tax.

khāṭir: inclination.

kullī: totality, whole and not in part.

ladhādha: pleasure.

ma'ānī: inward meaning corresponding to what is intended by the aṣl (Origin) as opposed to outward form (ṣūra).

mafāsid: (pl. of mafsada) what is harmful or not expedient, as opposed to what is beneficial or expedient (maṣlaḥa).

majāz: figurative interpretation as opposed to the interpretation by the evidence supported by the Text.

ma'lūl: as a philosophical term, it is generally translated as 'effect' as against cause ('illa); however, juristically it means what is inferred in a judgment (ḥukm) as a result of an 'illa (effective reasoning).

manafī: personal advantage or interest.

maqāṣid: (pl. of mqṣad), goals, objectives, purposes.

maṣāliḥ: (pl. of maṣlaḥa) see maṣlaḥa.

masḥ: cleaning three times around the neck during the process of ablution (wuḍū).

maṣlaḥa: what is beneficial or expedient.

maṣlaḥa al-mursala: a maṣlaḥa al-mursala, not explicitly supported by the Text (naṣṣ).

maṣlaḥa kullīiya: what is beneficial for the whole community.

mastūr: one having a blameless record.

mithl: same for same, as for example gold for gold.

mu'āmalāt: mutual relations (of Muslims with other nations).

mubāḥāt: (sing. mubāḥ) what is permissible.

mujāzā: mutual reciprocity.

mukallaf: subject to legal obedience.

munāsaba: affinity or suitability to the Text and textual evidence.

murā'āt al-khilāf: allowance for the disagreement in opinion.

mustā'min: anyone who has been given the promise of security or safe conduct by the Muslims.

mu'tabr qiyās: acknowledged qiyās.

mu'thir: what is effective as an 'illa (effective reasoning) in a given judgment (ḥukm).

muṭlaq: absolute.

muwāda'a: treaties and contracts.

nāfila: supererogatory.

naṣṣ: Text (Qur'ān), also used for Texts (Wordings) of Ḥadīth and fiqh.

qāḍī: judge.

qaṭ'ī: certain.

qawī: strong.

qiyās: analogy, doctrine of systematic reasoning which seeks the 'illa (effective reasoning) in a given judgment (ḥukm) on the basis of the Qur'ān, Sunna or ijmā'.

qiyās jalīy: qiyās based on an apparent or explicit 'illa.

qiyās al-khafī: qiyās based on an implicit or hidden 'illa.

qiyās al-ma'ānawī: systematic reasoning based on inward meaning.

ra'y: individual discretion by the jurist exercised in the legal reasoning.

sabab: cause or motive.

sabr al-taqsīm: the observation and classification, method of exclusion.

ṣadaqa: donation.

shar': Law.

ṣaum: fasting.

sharī'a: Laws in Islamic jurisprudence based on four sources, the Qur'ān, Sunna, ijmā' and qiyās.

shurūṭ: (sing. sharṭ) stipulations in the contract or treaty or in a given judgment (ḥukm).

ṣūrī: outward form as opposed to inward meaning (ma'ānī).

siyāsa: administrative state organizations and public institutions.

sunna: normative legal custom practiced in Medina, the second source of Islamic jurisprudence.

ta'abūd: obedience.

taḥsīnī: (pl.taḥsīniyāt) to adapt to what conforms to the accepted practice.

takhṣīṣ: particularization or restriction.

takhṣīṣ al-'illa: particularization or restriction of an 'illa (effective reasoning) in a given judgment (ḥukm) based on and connected with the aṣl (Origin).

ta'līl: inference (which results as a consequence of an 'illa exercised in the derivation of an indepedent judgment.

tarjīḥ: what is preferable, as a result of an 'illa (effective reasonig) exercised in the derivation of an indepedent judgment (ḥukm) by a jurist.

tarkhkhuṣ: legal concessions.

'urf: custom.

uṣūl or uṣūl al-fiqh: (sing. aṣl, Origin) roots, principles or the theoretical basis of Islamic jurisprudence.

Uṣūl mahūma: principles on which the one who does derive the independent judgment in legal matters based on the four sources of Islamic jurisprudence relies on imagination or an individual opinion.

waṣf: characteristic or quality.

wuḍū': ablution

umm al-walad: female slave who has borne a child to her owner.

ẓāhir: apparent, explicit.

zakāt: alms tax.

ẓann: speculation.

ẓannī: speculative.

BIBLIOGRAPHY

I- SARAKHSĪ'S WORKS:

Uṣūl al-Sarakhsī. 2 Vols. ed. Abū al-Wafā al-Afghānī. Beirut: Dār al-Ma'ārif, 1372 A.H./1954 A.D.

Mabsūṭ 30 Vols. Cairo: Dār al-Ma'ārif, 1324-31 A.H./1906-12 A.D.

Sharḥ al-Siyar al-Kabīr. 4 Vols. ed. Ṣalāḥuddīn al-Munajjid. Cairo: Dār al-Ma'ārif, 1324-30 A.H./1906-12 A.D.

Sharḥ al-Siyar al-Kabīr. 5 Vols. Cairo: Lajnat Iḥyā al-Ma'ārif al-Nu'mānīya, 1372 A.H./1954 A.D.

II- SHAYBĀNĪ'S WORKS:

Jāmī' al-Ṣaghīr. Printed on the margin of Abū Yūsuf. **Kitāb al-Kharāj.** Cairo: Būlāq, 1302 A.H./1884 A.D.

Kitāb al-Aṣl. 4 Vols. ed. Abū al-Wafā al-Afghānī. Hyderabad: Dā'irā al-Ma'ārif, 1972.

Al-Aṣl. Vol. I, **Kitāb al-Buyū' wa al-Salam.** ed. Shafīq Shiḥāta. Cairo: Maṭba'a Jāmi' al-Qāhira, 1954.

III- AUTOBIOGRAPHICAL LITERATURE ON SHARAKHSĪ'S LIFE:

Khalīfa, Ḥājī (Kātib Çelebi). **Kashf al-Ẓunūn.** Istambul: Maarif Matbassi, 1943.

Ṣalāḥuddīn al-Munajjid. **Kitāb al-Siyar al-Kabīr.** Vol. I. Cairo: Dār al-Ma'ārif, 1324-31 A.H./1908-13 A.D.

Laknawī, 'Abd al-Ḥaīy al-Hindī. **Kitāb al-Fawā'id al-Bahīya fī Tarājim al-Ḥanafīya.** Cairo: Printed by Aḥmad Nāgī al-Jamālī and Muḥammad Amīn Khānjī, 1914.

Mays, Khalīl. **Fahāris al-Mabsūṭ.** Beirut: Dār al-Ma'ārif, 1980.

Qurashī, Ibn Abū al-Wafā. **Jawāhir al-Muḍīya.** Hyderabad: Dā'ira al-Ma'ārif, 1980.

Quṭlūbughā, Ibn. **Tāj al-Tarājim fī Ṭabqāt al-Ḥanafīya.** Baghdad: Maktaba al-Muthannā, 1962.

IV- PRIMARY SOURCES:

'Abd al-Salām, 'Izz al-Dīn Sulmī. **Qawā'id al-Aḥkām fī Maṣāliḥ al-Anām.** Cairo: Maktaba al-Kullīyāt al-Azharīya, 1969.

Baṣrī, Abū al-Ḥusayn. **Kitāb al-Mu'atamad fī Uṣūl al-Fiqh.** Damascus: Isnstitute Français De Dames, 1964.

Būṭī, Muḥammad Sa'īd Ramḍān. **Ḍawābit al-Maṣlaḥa fī al-Sharī'a al-Islāmīya.** Damascus: al-Maktaba al-Umawīya, 1966-67.

Ghazālī, Abū Ḥāmid Muḥammad. **Al-Mustaṣfa min Uṣūl.** Baghdad: Maktaba al-Muthannā, 1970.

Ibn Ḥazm, Muḥammad 'Alī. **Iḥkām fī Uṣūl al-Aḥkām.** Vol. X. ed. Aḥmad Muḥammad Shākir. Cairo: Maktaba Khānjī, 1347 A.H./1928 A.D.

Isnawī, Jamāl al-Dīn. **Nihāya al-Su'al.** Printed on the margin of Ibn Amīr al-Ḥājj. **Al-Taqrīr wa al-Taḥbīr.** Cairo: Būlāq, 1317 A.H./1928 A.D..

Nasafī, 'Abd Allah ibn Aḥmad. **Manār al-Anwār, Manẓūmāt al-Kawākibī.** Cairo: Maṭba'a al-'Ilmīya, 1317 A.H./1899 A.D..

Qarāfī, Shihāb al-Dīn. **Tanqīḥ al-Fuṣūl fī Ikhtiṣār al-Maḥṣūl fī al-Uṣūl.** Cairo: Maktaba al-Kullīyāt al-Azharīya, 1961.

Rāzī, Fakhr al-Dīn. **Kitāb al-Maḥṣūl.** Cairo: Maṭba' al-Ḥasnīya, 1905.

Shāfi'ī, Muḥammad bin Idrīs. **Kitāb al-Umm.** Vol. VII. Cairo: Būlāq, 1331 A.H./1912 A.D.

Shāṭibī, Abū Isḥāq. **Al-I'tiṣām.** Cairo: Maṭba'a al-Manār, 1913.

____________________ **Al-Muwāfaqāt.** Egypt: Maṭba'a al-Salfīya, 1341 A.H./1922 A.D.

Subkī, Tāj al-Dīn. **Jāmī' al-Jawāmi'.** Printed on the margin of 'Abd al-Raḥmān Bannānī.... **alā matn Jāmi' al-Jawāmi'.** Cairo: Muṣṭafā Bābī, 1937.

Taftāzānī, Mas'ūd ibn 'Omar. **Sharḥ al-Talwīḥ 'alā al-Tawḍīḥ.** Cairo: Būlāq, Maktaba al-Kubrīya al-Amīrīya, 1318 A.H./1900 A.D..
Taymīyya, Aḥmad ibn al-Ḥalīm. **Majmū'āt al-Rasā'il was masā'il.** Cairo: Maṭba'a al-Manār, 1349 A.H./1930 A.D..

______________________________. "Ibn Taimiya's Autograph Manuscript. ed. George Makdisi. **Materials for the Study of Islamic Thought in Arabic and Islamic Studies in Honour of Hamilton A.R. Gibb.** Leiden: E.J. Brill, 1965.

Ṭūfī, Najm al-Dīn. "Bayān i'tibār al-Maṣlaḥa al-Aḥkām al-Mu'āmalāt." **Al-Manār.** Vol. IX.

IV-SECONDARY SOURCES:

Aghnides, Nicholas Prodomou. **Mohammadan Theories of Finance with an Introduction to Muhammadan Law and a Bibliography.** New York: AMS Press, 1969.

Coulson, N.J. **A History of Islamic Law.** Edinburgh: Edinburgh University Press, 1964.

Goldziher, Ignaz. "Das Princip des Istiṣḥāb in der muhammedanischen Geseztwissenschaft." **Gessammelte Schriften.** Band II. Hidesheim: G. Olms Verlag, 1968.

Kerr, H. Malcolm. **Islamic Reform: The Political and Legal Theories of Muḥammad 'Abdū and Rashīd Riḍā.** Berkeley: University of California Press, 1966.

______________. "Rashīd Riḍā and Islamic Reform: An Ideological Analysis." **The Muslim World.** Vol. L, No. 1.

Khadduri, Majid. **Islamic Jurisprudence, Shāfi'ī's Risāla.** Baltimore: The John Hopkins University Press, 1961.

______________. **The Islamic Law of Nations, Shaybānī's Siyar.** Baltimore: The John Hopkins University Press, 1966.

Kruse, Hans. "The Foundation of Islamic Jurisprudence (Muḥammad al-Shaybani- Hugo Grotius of the Muslims." **Pakistan Historical Society Journal.** Vol. III, Part, IV, 1955.

____________. "Al-Shaybani on International Instruments." **Pakistan Historical Society Journal.** Vol. I, Part I (1953).

Liebesny, Herbert J. "Religious Law and Westernization in the Moslem Near East." **American Journal of Comparative Law.** Vol. II. (1953).

Masud, Muhammad Khalid. **Islamic Legal Philosophy**. Islamabad: Islamic Research Instittute, 1977.

Ma'ṣūmī, Muḥammad Ṣaghīr Ḥasan. **Disagreements of the Jurists (Ikhtilāf al-Fuqhā').** Islamabad: Islamic Research Institute, 1965.

Schacht, Joseph. **The Origin of Muhammadan Jurisprudence.** London: Oxford University Press, 1950.

_______________. **Das Kitāb al-Makhārij fī al-Ḥayal des ImāmMuḥammad bin al-Shaybānī.** Leipzig: J.C. Heinrich's Buchhanlung, 1930.

V-WORKS USED FOR GENERAL REFERENCES:

The Encyclopaedia of Islam. Vols. I-IV, New Edition. Leiden: E.J. Brill, 1934-78.

Shorter Encyclopaedia of Islam. Ithaca, New York: Cornell University Press, 1965.

Ali, Yusuf. **The Holy Qur'ān.** Printed in U.S.A.: McGregor and Werner, 1934.

Al-Wāqidī. **Kitāb al-Maghāzī.** ed. Marsden Jones. London: Oxford University Press, 1966.

Ibn al-Athīr, Majd al-Mubārak. **Nihāya fī Gharīb al-Ḥadīth wa al-Athar.** Printed in Egypt: Maṭba'a al-'Uthmānī, 1893.

INDEX

extension (see tawassū'), 5, 18, 27, 28, 29, 48

external form (see also ṣūra), 26, 54

Facilitating, 18, 54, 55, 62

facilitation, 7, 23, 54

false (see also fāsid), 82

far' (see also branch of law), 73

Faraḥ (see also happiness), 87

Farghānā, 104, 105, 107, 110, 111

fāsid (see also invalid), 82

fasting (see also ṣaum), 35, 36, 37, 79, 91

figurative application or interpretation (see also majāz), 67, 83, 89

flexibility, 18, 22

fornication, 15

fuqhā' (scholars of Islamic jurisprudence), 25, 92

furū' (see also branches of law), 4, 37, 43, 87, 93, 103

General consensus (see also ijmā'), 2, 25, 26, 41, 60, 61, 67, 69, 70, 77, 79, 80, 86, 87

Ghazālī, Abū Ḥāmid Muḥammad, 62, 63, 65, 66, 72, 73, 75, 76, 90

ghulū', (exceeding beyond the bounds of sharī'a), 92

ghusal (washing of the body), 38

ground(s) (see also wujh and wujūh), 7, 33, 34, 38, 44, 50, 53, 64, 71, 81, 89

guardianship (see also walāya), 34, 38, 50

Ḥadd (see also punishment by divine law),

ḥadīth (see also tradition), 3, 4, 5, 16, 19, 22 , 23, 25, 51, 60, 80, 86, 96

ḥāja, ḥajāt (see also ḍarūra and necessity), 31, 58, 76, 89

ḥājī (needed), 91

Ḥājī Khalifa (Çelbi), 10, 12

Ḥajj (see also pilgrimage), 35

Halawānī, 'Abd al-'Azīz, 104, 105, 106, 107

Ḥambalī jurists, 63

Hambalī school of thought, 62, 68, 69, 94, 95, 98, 109

Ḥanafī jurists, 1, 28, 71, 87, 101

Ḥanafī school of thought, 3, 47, 48, 60, 61, 62, 64, 71, 73, 79, 92, 101

happiness, 87

Ḥasan, bin Mas'ūd, 109

ḥasr (restriction), 78

hawa (desire or inclination), 84

hereafter(s) (see also ākhira), 87

Prophet, 2, 5, 23, 25, 26, 41, 47, 50, 52, 77, 84, 106

protection (see also dhimma), 18, 29, 30, 51, 53, 55, 56, 57

public property, 54

purity and perfection, 24

Qaḍā', 36

Qāḍī, 23

Qarāfī, Shihāb al-dīn, 65, 88, 89

qaṭ'ī (see also certain), 65, 66, 70, 71, 78, 79, 82, 83, 86, 88, 90

qawī (see also strong), 23, 24, 25, 33, 36, 64, 69, 82, 89, 93

qiyās (doctrine of systematic reasonin)g, 2, 3, 4, 5, 6, 7, 14, 27, 28, 34, 40, 41, 43, 47, 49, 50, 53, 54, 58, 61, 62, 63, 64, 65, 67, 68, 69, 71, 72, 73, 75, 76, 95; its components, 73, 81, 83, 84, 86

qiyās khafī or jalīy (concealed qiyās), 63

qiyās lafzī (qiyās by wording), 81

qiyās ma'ānwī (qiyās by inward meaning), 67, 81

qiyās mu'atabar (acknowledged qiyās), 87

Qur'ān, 1, 2, 3, 4, 5, 19, 22, 23, 24, 25, 26, 27, 47, 52, 60, 62, 66, 67, 68, 72, 81, 87, 93

Ramḍān, 77

rationalists (see also ahl al-ra'y), 2, 14

ra'y (juristic reasoning), 1, 2, 3, 5, 6, 14, 16, 23, 24, 25, 26, 33, 47, 49, 60, 63, 65, 66, 68, 73, 94, 95, 97, 100, 102; as a methodology in the form of istisḥāb, 60; in the form of istiḥsān, 60; in the form of istiṣlāh, 26, 60, 61 ; in the form of qiyās, 26, 60

Rāzī, Fakhr al-dīn, 65, 66, 67, 74, 75, 76, 82, 88

reason, 70, 81, 88, 91

rebels, 4, 17, 18

rebuttal, 23, 81

reciprocity (see also mujāzā), 5, 7, 29. 30. 56

rectification (see also istidrāk), 67, 78

religion (dīn), 72, 91

religious affairs (see also aḥkām al-dīn), 2, 4, 6, 17, 28, 35, 44, 55, 69, 70, 74, 76, 80, 85, 92, 93, 94, 99

religious observances (see also 'ibādāt), 35, 77, 79, 91, 94, 95

religious sanctions, 26, 35

requital, 43

Riḍā, Rashīd, 68, 86, 90, 95, 97, 130

riwāya (chain of narration), 41, 105

rukū' (see also bowing), 35